CHARLES McKEAN

FIGHT BLIGHT

A practical guide to the causes of
urban dereliction and what
people can do about it

KAYE & WARD · LONDON

First published in Great Britain by
Kaye & Ward Ltd
21 New Street, London EC2M 4NT
1977

ISBN 0 7182 1150 2 (cased)
ISBN 0 7182 1169 3 (paper)

Photoset in VIP Palatino by
Western Printing Services Ltd, Bristol
Printed in Great Britain by
Whitstable Litho Ltd, Whitstable, Kent

CONTENTS

FOREWORD

We seem so unable to stop the rotting of our towns and cities or even to clean up the mess, that foreign visitors must have the same impression of us now that we had of the poorer Continental countries in the nineteen fifties and sixties (and we are now as dependent upon the tourist income as they were then). One sign of a poor country is the inability to clean up its front yard (to say nothing of its backyard) and that sign is now widespread in Britain.

Ironically, a good deal of the mess has not been caused by poverty, but by affluence. We had so much money that we soon picked up many ways of mis-spending it in a grand manner. We have demolished what was often good, and attempted to replace it by improvements. Instead, we have frequently replaced it with something far worse. Few people were consulted about the Brave New World foisted upon us, and few seem to like it. Consequently, a great number of books have been written to explain where we have gone wrong, and even more are published each month. But one's mind can become too clogged with theories.

This book is intended to be *practical*, showing what people have done to improve their environment, and how they did it. They are not supermen, but ordinary mortals who have achieved results from which other ordinary mortals might learn.

Some of the information in this book has been published elsewhere in different form. What has been attempted in this book, and which has not been adequately treated elsewhere, is the logical sequence of local involvement in the environment: starting with the inevitable fact of blight and dereliction, the occupation of land, the remedial works to improve morale, the supplementing of local authority programmes, up to the replacement of such programmes by local initiative. This book tries to show that local organisation has both the capability and responsibility to undertake such work. If successful, there would be two other vital consequences: firstly, more will be achieved for the same cost, and secondly, what is achieved is more likely to satisfy the consumers.

Acknowledgements

With grateful thanks to Colin Hines, Rob Arber, Pete Wilkinson (FOE) Annette Drago and Ed Berman (Inter-Action), Jim Monahan and Martin Coombes (CGCA), Eddie Hilton (Deputy Borough Planning Officer, Rochdale), Rod Hackney, Walter Segal, Chris Whittaker, Robert Howard, Max Hutchinson, Derek Pratt, Dickon and Charlotte Robinson, Judith Strong, Jenny Lewis, Tom Jestico, Cathy Davis, Chris Lakin, Alan Jeffrey, John McKean, the RIBA London Environment Group, Bernard Williams, Kay Beaumont, Mike Merchant, David Lock, Alex McCormick (without whom the book would not have been written), Margaret Yeo, Peter Murray, and the RIBA Eastern Regional Council for their support in developing the arguments in Chapter 9. Thanks, too, must go to all those individuals and organisations mentioned in the main text.

Photograph Acknowledgements

The author also wishes to thank the following for permission to reproduce photographs:
Arthur Hunt, p. 28; Alex Levac, pp. 45, 49; the Brick Development Association, p. 51; Jim Monahan, p. 75; Derek Pratt, pp. 82, 130; John McKean, p. 92; Fay Godwin, p. 94; Robert Howard, p. 95; Tom Jestico, p. 97; Rod Hackney, pp. 106, 107; M. B. Rochdale, pp. 123, 124; Planning Magazine, pp. 154, 155; and the Covent Garden Community Association, pp. 160, 161.

1 · SETTING THE SCENE

Decay in towns and cities is probably more prevalent now than it has been for decades; almost every High Street has a gap site caused by the demolition of a building, shops boarded up and covered in peeling flyposters, walls and buildings covered in graffiti. Just beyond the town centres, swathes of redevelopment areas are cordoned off by corrugated sheeting or chicken-wire fencing. We have become so used to seeing corrugated iron and advertisement hoardings that we have almost ceased to question why they are there. Yet behind them lie empty land or unused buildings, which ought to be available for use until redevelopment occurs. The first, and most important step in fighting this blight is a psychological one – that of realising that corrugated sheeting or fencing is not a permanent fixture: it can be removed and stacked on one side, to release the land beyond for use.

The fact that dereliction exists in such quantities may fairly be taken as a sign that the existing system is breaking down. E. M. Forster wrote a vivid short story called *The Machine Stops* in which he foresaw an age in which all people were totally dependent upon a complicated life-support machine. But it was unable to do one thing – which was to remedy a fault in its own works. There is a parallel with the way in which we have come to depend more and more on actions by the Government and local Councils. In the 'sixties, a problem only needed to be identified for cries of 'The Government must deal with this' to be uttered, and a new department set up. We have acquiesced as the authorities have absorbed more and more tasks that were once performed by communities or families – looking after the sick, the elderly, the homeless, the poor and other disadvantaged groups. This has

Few people questioned the quality of what the machine actually provided: The Red Road flats in Glasgow, the Corporation of which used to boast of having erected the 'highest flats in Europe' – these.

meant, as Martin Pawley suggests in his book *The Private Future*, that people have been able to immure themselves in very restricted worlds, gradually ceasing to take an interest in wider matters.

Comforting though it may have been to have the Government take the responsibility, few people seem to have assessed whether the quality of its actions, for which we have been paying, has been good enough, and the results – whether in Council housing or even in the way officialdom treats enquiries – leave a lot to be desired. We have become too dependent upon the machine: the magazine *Community Action* details in almost every issue some major campaign by tenants of one estate or another to pressure the Council to repair their homes, mend their broken windows, clean their stairs, or fill in the holes in the skirting-board. The financial relationships in Council housing can therefore mean that once a tenant is paying rent to the Council, he ceases to carry out for himself even the most simple task, such as mending a broken window. (Larger scale problems such as condensation, damp and inefficient heating systems are, however, an entirely different matter.)

There is little doubt that the machine *is* breaking down, and it is high time to question whether we have not asked too much of it, or whether it has not grabbed too much to itself. The analysis of blight and dereliction in the following chapters emphasises that dereliction is a *local* problem, and that action to change it can well be on a quite tiny scale – such as planting flowers in roadside verges and neglected patches of 'no man's land'. Surely this is work for the community, rather than the authorities?

There are those who favour changing the world from the top down, and those who prefer to tackle it from the bottom up. This book takes the latter view. It concentrates on what ordinary people have done, how they have done it and what lessons can be learnt from the doing. It is certain that if the recommendations of this book were to become widely practised, major changes would naturally follow. If people discover their own ability to affect their environment, they will no longer take kindly to being dominated by the authorities.

Most of the projects are small, but this means that they are practical; although small enough for communities throughout the country to imitate without too much risk, their combined effect, if widely practised, would be enormous.

Teddy Taylor, MP for Cathcart (Glasgow) wrote in *The Guardian* of a speech he had prepared for the residents of a local modern out-of-town Council estate, on subjects ranging from the Common Market to devolution. Each argument 'had been carefully prepared, and I had wrestled with each word. But question time, when it came, concentrated almost exclusively on the issue of dustbins. . . . What's the point of extending democracy if the democracy we have can't solve the real problems which affect the lives of real people today? Like dustbins and vandals.'

2 · BLIGHT AND ITS CAUSES

In this book, blight is taken is its widest possible context to mean dereliction *of any sort* in villages, towns or cities. Generally, dereliction is caused by neglect, and neglect can occur either whilst areas are awaiting redevelopment, or by simple carelessness. Most neglect is, however caused by the delay or slow implementation of rebuilding proposals, and therefore a large part of this chapter deals with causes of delay.

Gardeners' blight, is defined by the dictionary as similar to 'nipped in the bud' or 'wither' and it has certain significant parallels with the progress of urban decay. This can be seen particularly in the way in which the life drains from neglected communities, as shops, pubs, and other facilities close down, and houses are bricked up. The *official* meaning of blight is very much more restricted, and is referred to in the 1971 Town and Country Planning Act (Section 192 and following) which provides that where an owner is unable to sell his property at a reasonable price by reason of a planning proposal, he can compel the local Council or the Government to purchase his property at its full market value (assessed as though no planning proposal existed) by serving them with a 'blight notice'. Thus this important provision only deals with the limited subject of compensation to owners.

DELAY IN IMPLEMENTATION OF LOCAL AUTHORITY PLANS

The effect of Development Plans and Long-term Development Proposals

The 1947 Town and County Planning Act required local and

The process of urban decay. This part of Vauxhall, London, has been in this condition for some years.

County Councils to prepare development plans for their respective areas, and they were given power to declare Comprehensive Development Areas (CDA's – nicknamed in some cities such as Glasgow as Comprehensive *Demolition* Areas). CDA's were originally devised to cope with bomb-damaged areas and Councils could purchase compulsorily for redevelopment areas of decaying buildings or inadequate road pattern (and also purchase neighbouring 'added lands' if this would make the new development more efficient). The declaration of CDA's attracted specific Government finance and subsidy, and this proved to be an incentive to local Councils to use this power. Indeed, some authorities went overboard in their enthusiasm; the city of Glasgow, for example, declared twenty-nine such CDA's.

The effects of CDA's were, and still are, dramatic. The future of the areas thus designated becomes uncertain; no new businesses are started up, the buildings are neglected, owner-occupiers find it difficult to sell if they wish to move house, and the local Council frequently ceases to maintain the area, on the grounds that such expenditure is wasted if it is to be demolished. Consequently, the locality can deteriorate into an appalling slum, and thus, in a *post hoc* way, justify the Council's original designation. As often as not, buildings and streets of character could be pulled down because they stood in the way of a more 'efficient' layout of streets and 'blocks of housing'. Only recently has it been realised that much inner-city employment was, traditionally, in businesses with less than six employees, low overheads and in old buildings. When development arrived, a very high percentage of these firms closed down altogether rather than relocate elsewhere. This is a major contributory cause of unemployment in inner areas.

A prime cause of blight, however, is not the redevelopment itself, but the length of time it takes a local Council to acquire all the buildings and demolish them, during which time the area decays, becoming derelict, vandalised and dangerous.

'According to the Henney Report (A review for the Department of the Environment of the building programmes in Britain's big cities, principally London) a substantial proportion of the dwellings demolished in the euphoria of "rebuilding London" were not sub-standard at all, and need not have been knocked down. It says that about 60 per cent of the houses demolished between 1967 and 1972 had been classified in 1967 of being in "good or fair" condition. The cost of replacing them then turned out to be time-consuming, expensive and inefficient.' (*The Sunday Times*, 22 August 1976)

Hutchesontown was an area just south of the River Clyde in inner Glasgow, which was developed in the late eighteenth century as a speculative development of the rising middle and professional classes. Splendid large stone houses were constructed along wide streets such as Abbotsford Place, but over the years, along with the neighbouring Gorbals, the area lost its class, and the buildings became over-occupied and decayed. The awful reputation of the Gorbals, coupled with the fact that soot had coloured the stone buildings black, inspired the City Corporation to declare a CDA. Total demolition of these houses ensued, and they have now been replaced by tower blocks. I visited the last house to be demolished and it was clear from inside that firstly the building was sound; secondly it had never been subdivided as we had read in the newspapers and thirdly, that its last occupier had maintained his splendid rooms with great care. On coming out of this building, I was accosted by an old man who claimed to be the last original inhabitant of the district; they had not knocked his house down because it was propping

The last houses of Hutchesontown, Glasgow, with their replacements looming on the right.

up a nearby railway arch. 'I have lived my whole life here,' he said, 'there was a time when you could buy anything you needed in the whole of your life between Abbotsford Place and the river without needing to go into the town. There was a real community. Now you can't even buy a bottle of milk, it's a half hour walk for the wife to the nearest shop and that's going to close soon.'

Clerkenwell is one of London's ancient villages, once famous for its specialist clock and watch makers. When Huguenots were forced out of France in the late seventeenth century they came to Spitalfields, just east of the city, and to Clerkenwell where some original Huguenot weavers cottages still remain. Since 1960, some of them have been standing on a site programmed for a school extension for the Inner London Education Authority. In November 1975, the ILEA declared the land surplus to requirements; and although a conservation area has been declared at last, the buildings are so badly decayed that one collapsed in early 1976.

New Motorways and Major Roads

Most town and cities in the United Kingdom have been and still are under some pressure to reorganise the roads systems from

Sometimes these Ring Roads did not encircle cities but went right through the middle. The historic High Street of Glasgow is still threatened with. . .

their old patterns into ones which can cope with today's traffic. Councils could not pay the entire cost of these motorways, and 75 per cent of the cost is met by the Government. Serious and widespread blight can arise where a Council makes a proposal for new motorways, ring roads or other major roads, without the finance to go ahead, and in the current financial situation it is unlikely that the Government is going to approve more major schemes. But despite this, Councils still safeguard the proposed routes by preventing new developments along them instead of lifting the threat and abandoning the idea. Thus many properties are still affected by possible road developments even though the money to construct them may not be available for many years.

Generally ring roads were misnomers, for more often than not they were routed right through the centre of towns. In Bristol a dual carriageway cut its way between the seventeenth-century Christmas Steps area and

this.

the mediaeval St John's Gate; in Glasgow, a ring motorway is still planned to sail up ancient High Street, demolishing in its path a 1751 Episcopalian Chapel, and the only surviving villa designed by Robert Adam as part of a unique development in Charlotte Street. Indeed, Glasgow Corporation's plans were so grandiose that they were proposing to construct more motorway miles per head of population than any other major conurbation in Britain or Europe, although the city had one of the lowest car ownership rates.

Many of these new roads were used to restructure the towns and cities through which they were driven, in that all other development was planned around them; and one such road is Nottingham's Maid Marion

A similar result in Nottingham. The bottom of Maid Marion Way, with the car park, and blank face of the Broadmarsh Centre on the right have together transformed this historic area (the castle is just visible above the car park). Note the anti-personnel pavement.

Way, which is a dual carriageway running in a north/south direction through the centre, whose destruction caused the demolition of several fine historic buildings such as the Collins Almshouses. The historic streets of Nottingham run in an east/west direction from the castle to the Parish Church of St Mary's, and thus Maid Marian Way cut right across them with the result that several of these ancient routes – such as Castlegate, Warser Gate and St James's Street have become almost economic cul-de-sacs. Only Friar Gate, which is provided with a pedestrian tunnel underneath Maid Marian Way, still retains its former vitality.

Road Widenings

Instead of spending money purchasing the land required for road widenings, Councils usually insist that new buildings are set back a required distance from the old building line. This process, known as the 'if and when' policy, has not only damaged historic streets (a good example of this can be seen in Tottenham Court

Road in London) but casts a blight over the older properties in the street.

In 1969 the GLC published an explanatory book entitled seductively *Tomorrow's London* to accompany their Greater London Development Plan (GLDP). The concluding paragraphs of this book stated 'The time is not far off when the buildings of our main east/west axis from Aldgate Pump to Notting Hill Gate will have to come down, when we may have to have a new north/south line from Euston to Charing Cross.' I spent an enjoyable but incredulous day in the Historic Buildings division of the GLC calculating the damage these proposals would cause; and allowing perhaps 50 ft on either side of this east/west route from Aldgate Pump to Notting Hill Gate, the demolition included (among hundreds of other buildings listed by the Government of being of special architectural or historical interest) two mediaeval churches, three Wren churches, the Royal Exchange, the Mansion House, the Old Bailey, the new Czecho-slovak Embassy, Marble Arch, all of Oxford Street including Selfridges and Centre Point, Staple Inn, the Prudential Insurance headquarters and Holborn Viaduct.

In November 1962, London's famous Coal Exchange in lower Thames Street was demolished in some haste, despite wide-spread protests, for a road widening proposal. The Exchange had been designed in 1846 by J. B. Bunning, and was regarded as 'the prime city monument of the early Victorian period'. Fifteen years later, most of the site is still empty and derelict.

There are two syndromes to which traffic planners are particularly prone: the self-fulfilling prophecy, and the pneumonia syndrome. The self-fulfilling prophecy takes the form of the prediction of an impending crisis together with a proposed remedy, but the latter in fact precipitates the crisis. In this case, traffic congestion is diagnosed, and new road space or road widening is proposed as as cure, but this 'cure' will attract new cars on the roads and thus cause greater congestion than before. The pneumonia syndrome, which is similar, is the planner's equivalent of a doctor who, unable to find a cure for the common cold, allows the patient to develop pneumonia for which he *does* know the remedy. (From an unpublished RIBA report on the GLDP 1971.)

Slum Clearance Procedures

The slum clearance procedures of the Housing Act 1957 (part 3) permit the local Council to acquire for demolition all residential properties represented by the Medical Officer of Health (MOH)

An apt comment in Lambeth, London.

as being unfit for human habitation. Originally the Council was compelled to demolish such houses and rebuild on the site, but the Act has been amended recently to allow Councils to rehabilitate the houses instead. Part 5 of this Act deals more generally with sub-standard areas which could be demolished and developed more efficiently, usually with some change in the road layout and disposition of buildings. Controversy has been caused by the fact that a house could be demolished on the representations of the MOH or the Sanitary Inspector even though such officials are trained only in health matters, and not in the structural state of buildings.

Community Action magazine reports:

In September 1973 a public enquiry was held into the future of the Ladybarn area of Manchester, and the Inspector's report, stated that some 72 houses classified as unfit by the local Council did not warrant it and more than 111 more were capable of improvement. The Inspector stated in his report 'Although some of the houses were not free from defect, there are others that are in such a condition that it is difficult to understand why they were ever included in the clearance area by the Council.'

DELAY IN THE PROGRAMME

Some Councils, with programmes of redevelopment which out-stripped either the available finance or political reality, may find themselves owners of unoccupied property or land without the resources to develop; and some are continuing, even now, to purchase privately owned property without having the money to rehabilitate or demolish. The result is that properties lie empty, with their windows bricked or boarded up. A situation probably caused by two different departments not knowing what the other one is up to; one purchasing the property, and the other without the funds to repair it.

The GLC (GLC Report 25th March 1976), states that 'In future, our major improvement panel will concentrate its efforts on schemes for the improvement of estates and not on acquired properties.' Surely, in that case, it should stop continuing to acquire them?

The lengthy time-table of some of the more grandiose schemes in itself can also cause delay.

The GLC (Report 3 June 1976) states that, assessed on the basis of interest charges, two thirds of the time scale of a development occurs before construction begins, and that this time scale can be particularly long when dealing with inner city sites and multiple and spread ownerships. Although this report claims that internal action will be taken to reduce this preliminary delay, it is worth noting some of the bureaucratic pro-cesses which contribute to it. Take, for example, a standard application for housing development which goes to a London Borough. There are well over ten stages which include the following: (*a*) preparation of the planning brief and consultation; (*b*) planning brief to architects depart-ment or to consultant architects; (*c*) preparation of the housing brief by the housing department; (*d*) the sketch plan from the architects back to the housing and planning department; (*e*) the sketch plan to the DoE; (*f*) DoE approval and comments; (*g*) back to the housing development sub-committee; (*h*) application for full planning permission and public participation; (*i*) the scheme goes out to tender; (*j*) committee approval required for the tender.

One of Glasgow's many Comprehensive Development Areas – a typical scene that could have been taken in most districts of the city. That the area is still inhabited can be judged from the washing hanging out to dry.

The Covent Garden Association points out that development in that area has to be firstly approved by the Greater London Council's Covent Garden Committee, Finance and Scrutiny Committee, then probably the Policy and Resources Committee, the Central Area Board, and the Historic Buildings Board where required; consultation is also required with similar committees in the City of Westminster and the London Borough of Camden since they have powers over this area, and, finally, permission (particularly if housing is involved) must be obtained from the DoE. This is hardly a procedure which will encourage dynamic action!

A vivid (if appalling) example of the results of this is described in the book *The Evangelistic Bureaucrat* by Jon Gower Davis. The Rye Hill area of Newcastle – an area of poorly maintained but soundly constructed houses – was being purchased by the Council for eventual rehabilitation. The length of this process and the rippling effect of having more and more buildings being bricked up, led to the area being vandalised and the buildings themselves decaying to such a state that they had to be demolished. To some degree or other much the same process has occurred in every town and city in Britain.

Lack of Urgency

Council redevelopment programmes are frequently characterised by a lack of urgency:

The GLC has owned the Bell Hotel site in Covent Garden for 10 years, during which time they have delayed rebuilding on various grounds, the excuse usually given being that they would like to redevelop the adjacent buildings as well. However, that there is little urgency in their plans can be judged from this entry in the GLC minutes (4 May 1976) 'For the Bell Hotel site, pre-brief sketches have been shown to the (Covent Garden) Forum and the complete brief is expected in July.' In other words, years after buying the site, pre-brief sketches have been prepared; a complete brief is not expected for a further three months. The Arabs think differently: they have been known to commission projects one hundred times the size of the Bell Hotel site, and require the builder to start on site within three months – all design work complete!

Lack of Political Will and Political Indecision

Since councillors like to be liked, they can be chary of taking unpopular decisions – so much so, that not to take a decision is fast becoming policy with some Councils. Sometimes excuses for not giving a decision are based on the lack of a current development plan, in view of which any decision is considered premature or piecemeal. Decisions can also be deferred when councillors agree to designate some part of their territory as a General Improvement Area (GIA) or a Housing Action Area (HAA), but are unwilling to devote the necessary funds to carrying out the housing rehabilitation work. Although much of the work is aided by grants from the DoE, they would rather forfeit such grants than spend some of their own money to match them.

A prospective buyer recently approached Norfolk County Council about a cottage in their ownership in Norwich which was derelict. The Council refused to sell the property, stating that they were uncertain of the use to which it would be put. In fact it was never used and in due course was demolished.

An example of political indecision on a wide scale is the large tract of land lying behind the Angel, Islington, much of which has been cleared for many years, and the remainder of which is derelict. The Council had zoned the area for a combination of open space, and a new shopping and commercial development, all of which were to have been allied to a gigantic traffic roundabout. A complete lack of a realistic time-table has meant that the land which could have been fully used on a temporary basis over many years has been frozen, empty, and dirty on the grounds of the perpetually imminent development.

FURTHER BUREAUCRATIC DELAYS

Inter-Departmental and Authority Clashes

Delays, differences of opinion and lack of communication between the departments of the same Council and between separate authorities can cause blight and decay, and the GLC, for example, in their assessment of delays, note that negotiations with London boroughs was one of the prime causes. The two examples which follow can be taken as representative of a widespread problem:

An historic building in central London has a valuable early eighteenth-century carved wooden staircase which is listed as a monument of architectural and historic interest. During rehabilitation negotiations, the Fire Officer has insisted that the staircase be boarded with asbestos. The Historic Buildings officials will not permit this on the grounds that this would ruin the staircase. Neither side is giving in – the result is stalemate.

An empty site in Hampstead, within a conservation area, has been scheduled for a small block of residential flats. The planners say the block must be at least four storeys tall in order to match the character of the surrounding area. Unfortunately the DoE recently ruled that families with children must only be in ground-floor maisonettes and that nobody should have to walk up more than two flights of stairs. This makes a three-storey building. Unfortunately again, subsidy is not forthcoming to provide lifts in developments as small as this. Since for perfectly valid conservation reasons, the planners will not permit a three-storey building, and the DoE will not pay for a four-storey building, there is a total impasse.

Taking the Easy Way Out

Many Councils have become too used to thinking in terms of

large cleared sites which can be easily developed. Indeed, where there is pressure on a Council to erect as many houses as quickly as possible without too much regard for their quality, the architect might find it easier to arrange a contractor's package deal for a thousand houses on a large site, rather than become involved in the preparation of rehabilitation proposals. He is less vulnerable to the politicians at committee level with the larger scheme, since the politicians themselves use house building figures for re-election. Many Councils, therefore, regard some sites as difficult to redevelop (such as those on which Walter Segal will be constructing his houses in Lewisham – see Chapter 6) and despite the fact that, as often as not, houses used to exist on them, such sites are frequently too small or ill-shaped to fit neatly into a local authority's programme. Perhaps even the Government's own cost controls over housing restrict the use to which difficult sites might be put.

Derelict urban land and unused pockets inside the suburbs are neglected in favour of country sites. Merseyside was the first authority to commission Dr Alice Coleman to produce a land use map of urban fringe areas. 'We compared 1963 patterns with present, and we found that in 1963 there had been 24 square kilometres which were predominantly waste or derelict. In the next decade Merseyside built new settlements on 18 square kilometres but only half of this on disused land; the rest was on viable farmland.' (*The Sunday Times*, 2 May 1976.)

London Borough of Hammersmith has a similar attitude to small sites. In a letter (30 September 1975) written by the assistant Director of Planning, the following information was given: 'There are about 54 vacant sites throughout Hammersmith covering an area of nearly 50 acres. Most of the sites are very small, being less than one third of an acre, and as such are really only viable as amenity open spaces.'

The cleared site mentality has permeated local Councils, the Government and private developers without distinction. In 1970, the Home Office made a proposal to demolish all the buildings between Bridge Street (Westminster) and Richmond Terrace, and replace them with a purpose-designed single Home Office building facing Whitehall. During the enquiry it transpired that the brief to the architects had been to consider the entire area as a cleared site – thus ignoring that there were 14 structures on the site listed as being of architectural or historic interest. One of these structures was New Scotland Yard (architect: Norman

Scene in Rotherhithe.

Shaw) which was listed Grade 1, that is to say that it is a building 'of such importance that its destruction in no case should be allowed'.

OFFICIAL NEGLECT THROUGH DISINTEREST

Left-over Areas

Officially there is no such designation as 'left-over areas' (LOA's); but they have come to exist as a consequence of officialdom's delight in pigeon-holing problems. The DoE has devised what it grandly calls its total approach to housing. At the bottom there are Comprehensive Development Areas, followed by the new 'gradual renewal' policy in Housing Action Areas, and in the adjacent Priority Areas, followed by the General Improvement Areas in which most houses will be saved and rehabilitated, and once again followed by the Conservation Area in which most things are so nice that they ought to be preserved. There is no designation to cover recently redeveloped areas (RRA's) nor for those places which are not so appalling as to require immediate

Creeping decay and dereliction in Nottingham. Many of the houses on the left are empty.

attention but which are, nevertheless, pretty miserable places to inhabit. Since they are not designated as anything, nobody in authority has any reason to study them, and their condition is likely to deteriorate until they are all discovered by some social research worker and blown up into a political scandal.

Intermediate Areas

This is not an official designation either, but may be applied to those commercial areas which happen to fall between other designated districts: they may not yet have suffered redevelopment, nor have been elevated to the status of a conservation area. they are thus deemed (in a very unspectacular sort of way) *expendable*.

One such area is the centre of the West End's rag trade – around Mortimer and Great Titchfield Streets – which is more or less surrounded by conservation areas. This district is neglected, and is gradually being eaten away by unrelated new development.

Ground level conditions of a Council estate. It could be anywhere, but is in fact in Bedford.

Sink Estates

This is a pejorative term applied to a Council housing estate (or to a housing district) in which problem families are concentrated. Far from receiving the additional care and attention they require, such estates are allowed to stew in their own juices. They become decayed and vandalised, miserable not only for their inhabitants but also for the neighbours; and insurance companies usually insist any shops in such areas cover their windows with metal shutters at night. Neglect and alienation feed on themselves, leading to the development of appalling social problems.

NEGLECT BY OFFICIAL BODIES

Official bodies such as British Rail, the army, the electricity, gas and water authorities are all major landholders and all seem to be as careless with their land as any local Council or private developer. For example, the rail system was constructed when the railways were healthier than they are now, and the sight of unused tracts of land of varying sizes alongside railway lines is common.

In many cities, British Rail owns a spectacular amount of land which lies derelict and unused. This can be seen in North London, East Bristol, or South Glasgow. In addition to old shunting yards and unused lines, in most towns the railway lines go through cuttings or over embankments, and more often than not the banks of these are neglected and become unofficial refuse tips. British Rail are also very poor custodians of their own heritage, and are the possessors of railway stations which are suffering from neglect, such as the magnificent Victorian tiled station at Worcester (Shrub Hill), the fine barge-boarding and wrought iron of the stations in South London – particularly Denmark Hill and Battersea, and the atmospheric little station at Milngavie, Scotland.

The Port of London Authority has been the owner of thousands of acres in London's dock land, and during the lengthening period of indecision about their development, the authority has been prejudicing future development by permitting rubbish tipping in the dock basins, which is filling them in. This does provide an income to the authority, but wastes a splendid asset that could be well put to use in the future.

In summary, there appears to be little pressure on public and official bodies to assess, periodically, their land-holding and ascertain what is surplus. Such bodies are always loath to give up land in case it might at some time in the future come in useful, and unfortunately, there is no compulsion on them to use the land beneficially during the interim period. It is possible that British Rail's acceptance of the City Farms (see Chapter 4) heralds a change in attitude.

NEGLECT BY PRIVATE OWNERS

Unused Private Gardens and Land

There is a surprisingly large number of empty gardens, tennis courts, recreation grounds and cemeteries which could well be put to use. There is nothing deliberate about this waste and proposals for dealing with it are discussed in Chapter 4.

Changing Social Patterns

Few people visiting such splendid buildings as the Royal Agricultural Hall (Islington) or the Covent Garden Flower Market a hundred years ago, could have conceived that they would become so obsolete that the Councils would have to advertise in the press for suggestions as to how they might be used. A hundred years before that, nobody would have questioned the future of mills or maltings; in mediaeval times the future of abbeys or even, in the nineteen thirties, the future of the glistening new cinemas or ancient parish churches. Indeed, habits change so quickly that only fifteen years ago, during the period of the so-called 'white heat of technology', few people would have thought it worth while thinking about new uses for such buildings. Nevertheless, despite the revived interest in re-using them there are many which are left empty and derelict, because their conversion would present too many problems for the Councils, and too little economic return for the developers.

Development in the Wrong Place

Many new developments are becoming derelict because they are too far from town centres, or are simply too unattractive. They remain unoccupied, decaying and attracting vandalism and litter. They are usually the result of poor pre-planning.

Part of the Greyfriars Development in Ipswich may have to be demolished, since few tenants have been found to occupy it. Equally, the much less obtrusive Bell Court shopping centre in Stratford-on-Avon is in financial trouble because only three out of the twenty-eight shops are occupied. The planners are worried that if more effort is made to attract shops to Bell Court, the main shopping street will suffer. The Anderston Centre in Glasgow has never been fully occupied, and those who planned it now admit it was a mistake.

Historic Buildings

Some developers pay scant regard to the quality of the buildings on the site which they wish to develop, and when their plans are refused permission, the existing buildings on the site are often permitted to decay through casual or deliberate neglect, and, in time, reinforce the case for development. A pointer to such a proposed development is the empty house with its windows left open in all weathers.

The Sunday Times (8 August 1976) gives details of a proposal by Labour Party Properties to demolish part of a fine Regency terrace facing Walworth Road (South London) and replace it by a neo-Georgian block containing 20,000 sq. ft. of office space. This scheme has been delayed because the buildings were deservedly listed as being of historic interest.

Delays Caused by Negotiation

Usually it has been possible for developers to find out what the local Council will permit to be built on a given site. But there is always room for negotiation. On the one hand, developers may press for an over-development of the site, in the hope that as a result of bargaining they will still finish with more than if they had simply followed the guidelines. On the other hand, the Councils press for what they call 'planning gain'; this means simply that the developer provides the Council, free of charge, with something for which the Council would otherwise have to pay – such as flats, or a bit of open space, or a riverside walkway. It is doubtful that the originators of the British Town Planning Acts ever dreamt that the legislation could cause such squalid bartering. Sometimes such negotiations can lead to success, sometimes they can be influenced by the area in question being allowed to fall derelict, and sometimes the developer pulls out, leaving the site blighted. Such bartering can continue for years.

The Cost of Development

The present recession has brought with it the spectacle of the impoverished developer. With interest rates at about 14 per cent, the developer needs to make about a 3 per cent return of capital, any development has to produce a net return of at least 17 per cent which is nowadays unlikely. A great deal of land, then, which was bought when money was cheaper and planning permissions given more rapidly, is now lying derelict.

The City Planning Officer of Liverpool assessed in July 1976 that 600 acres of the city's territory, for which planning permission for development had already been, granted, were lying derelict. He considered that the reason for this was that the developers were waiting for land prices to rise again.

'Trammell Crow have pulled out of the proposed Trade Mart on the site of the Surrey Docks, London. . . . They say that until such time as there is a significant improvement in the general investment climate and a substantial fall in the level of interest rates they will defer the development timetable.' *Planning* 19.11.76.

OTHER CAUSES OF BLIGHT AND NEGLECT

The Effect of Modern Developments Elsewhere

The central area of a town is more than the sum of its functions that is, of entertainment, recreation, leisure commerce, and shopping. Consequently any attempt to suck these activities from the centre into new purpose-built complexes elsewhere is likely to do more than change the economic pattern – it could have the effect of changing the life of the centre itself.

In Nottingham two enormous new shopping centres have been constructed – the Victoria centre to the north and the Broadmarsh centre to the south. The result is that the vitality has disappeared from many of the historic streets, and empty shops in Goose Gate display signs in the windows saying 'moved to Broadmarsh centre'. It is feared that Ipswich will suffer a similar fate, for planning permission has been given for a hypermarket to the west of the town.

The Image of the City

The way in which a city develops largely reflects the image of it held by councillors and the officers. For example, many towns were thought to be old fashioned, and so massive shopping centres, town centre schemes, and motorways were pursued, usually to the detriment of any historic character and interest. Gloucester, Ipswich, Edinburgh, Nottingham and Manchester had their centres rebuilt; by chance the recession has saved Carlisle, Chesterfield and Cardiff. Councillors also like to be remembered by the number of houses built during their tenure of office, or by having new roads, parks or shopping precincts named after them.

A good way in which the image of a place can affect its future can be seen in Nottingham, where posters in the station advertise the town as the 'Queen of the Midlands' and 'Heart of the Industrial Midlands'. If Nottingham is regarded primarily as an industrial centre, one might suspect that short shrift would be given to its historic core and until very recently this was so. In other words, the preservation of historic buildings was considered incompatible with the image of a bustling industrial centre.

Malcolm MacEwen recalls that when he was campaigning in the Gorbals in Glasgow before the war, all the talk was of pulling down the entire area – not solely because it was necessarily unsafe, unfit or overcrowded, but also because the buildings were soot-blackened and looked awful from the outside.

There is a row of early nineteenth-century semi-detached Regency houses called the Paragon in Hackney, East London. Special features include colonnaded porches, a Greek key design in stucco and peculiar – almost triangular – windows above the door. In Greenwich, Hampstead or Kensington these buildings would be listed as being of historic interest, rehabilitated and occupied. In Hackney they are empty and likely to be demolished.

Zoning

As a reaction to the squalid Victorian conditions, such as in Bermondsey where houses were jammed against paint and glue factories, tanneries, chemical works and sewers, planning legislation enjoined Councils to zone their territories into separate activities and uses. However, planners have gone too far in the other direction, putting housing estates on one side of the town, industrial estates on the other, some commercial buildings in the centre, so separating out all the intertwined strands of life. Not only does this decrease the vitality of towns and cities, but it also increases the amount of travelling which people have to do to reach their work and entertainment. Also the fact that tremendous advances have been made on rendering industrial processes less noxious is ignored. The blighting effect of zoning can be seen wherever small works or industries are forced from their original locations because they are not in the correct zone; also since town centres are usually zoned as commercial it becomes very difficult to protect residential accommodation in them, because the land values rise. A different form of zoning has been reported by the magazine *Roof*, which describes cases where Building Societies have refused to advance mortgages for buildings in certain areas of some towns because of their 'unsuitability'. This will make it difficult to sell houses in these areas, which could decline very quickly as a result.

Unmannerly Neighbours

Decay and dereliction can be caused by the proximity of a nuisance, and it is interesting that much more fuss is made over the proposal for some new nuisance, than is ever made about an existing nuisance. The most obvious examples of the latter are motorways and airports, and the extent of the nuisance is only usually appreciated by those who have to live near them. A year ago Hounslow Council had to sell a recently completed school building because aircraft noise rendered it virtually unusable for teaching. Several departments of London University which occupied premises facing Gower Street, have had to stop using the rooms facing the street because the traffic noise and vibration greatly exceeded the maximum recommendations of the Government Report on noise (1963 Wilson Report). It is fair to assume that hundreds of miles of streets in London alone would have conditions similar to those in Gower Street.

The Backside of Modern Developments

A walk through almost any new central area will reveal the extent to which modern buildings have an unpleasant backside to them – a grandly titled 'service area' with a long, high, featureless wall of brick or stained concrete punctuated by large vehicle entrances with broken kerbs, pools of oil, yellow no-parking lines, dustbins and litter. In many historic towns such entrances destroy the streets entirely, and although opinions may differ about the

The brave new world of the Aylesbury estate in South London. The confetti-like substance on the road is broken glass.

beauty of the façade of the buildings, there is usually unanimity about the appearance of the service areas.

Cost of Blight

There are no national figures available to show the cost of blight, and the available figures refer only to sites whose owners are known – as opposed to the acres of no man's land. Two examples will have to be taken as representative:

The GLC's 1976–77 Budget includes a provision for £8 million debt charges on land which has been purchased but on which development has not yet begun. It estimates that the gross figures before Government subsidy will be £10,700,000 to 1977, £11,200,000 to 1978, and the same for the following year. The GLC hopes to reduce this figure but warns that this will only be achieved by substantial internal reorganisation.

The *Evening Standard* (18 May 1976) reported on 6.7 acres of land just north of Chiswick High Road and west of the Turnham Green Underground, which cost Hounslow Council £656,000 to buy and another

£10,000 to clear. The site has already been empty for over two years, and the annual interest charge is £70,000.

EXTENT OF BLIGHT

Any assessment of the extent of blight depends on the definition of blight which is used. However, in 1974 the Professional Institution's Council for Conservation assessed the amount of nationally derelict land at 135,000 acres. This is likely to be a gross underestimate since it does not include all land and buildings currently wasted. From time to time, the Friends of the Earth make their own rough and ready surveys of unused land, and their detailed reports on Newcastle-upon-Tyne and North Staffordshire have been published, together with assessment of the potential of actual sites. However, their assessments are based on land which is already cleared. If one added in no man's land, as described in the next chapter, unpleasant environments, decaying buildings and empty areas, then the total acreage would be really startling.

Of interest
Off the Rails. The SAVE Organisation's report on British Rail, its buildings and its land. £1.00.

3 · WHAT CAN BE DONE ABOUT BLIGHT?

Neither the Government nor the local Councils really approve of blight or dereliction (officially at least), and Councils have now been given powers of acquiring houses for social ownership as long as they come within certain categories, which include 'the acquisition of properties which have been left empty for at least two months in areas in which there is a serious shortage of housing, or where the purpose of acquisition is to relieve homelessness'. The compulsory acquisition of empty property is not a new idea. In days when robbers, bandits, wolves and bears ranged hungrily outside defensive city walls land was at a premium, and one learns of towns where the Councils could requisition empty property without compensation. Thomas Pennant, the eighteenth-century naturalist and traveller, discovered this when he was in Glasgow:

'The Dean of Guild can order any old houses to be pulled down that looked dangerous; and, I think, has also power in some places, of disposing, to the best bidder, ground of any houses which the owner suffers to lie in ruin for 3 years without attempting to rebuild.'

The difference between this account of Glasgow, and the new powers given to local Councils is that the latter have to pay full market price and occupy the premises themselves, whereas the Dean of Guild in Glasgow could merely act as an agent to promote action.

These new powers are largely valueless in practice, since the majority of blight in towns is probably caused by local Councils through themselves (see Chapter 2). Moreover there are strict limitations upon what the Council might buy: Wandsworth Council was refused permission to buy some new private houses, which could not be sold successfully on the market, because they had two bathrooms – too luxurious for public money; and yet Camden Council has had great difficulty in acquiring flats which were designed for company directors in Centre Point, because they did not fulfil the minimum standards of Council housing!

Major developments in towns and cities are not new. Haussman ploughed boulevards through densely inhabited districts of Paris, and in London less spectacular but possibly equally disastrous new roads were Charing Cross Road, Kingsway and Regent Street; and the Victorian railway engineers drove their lines right to the heart of British cities, as at St Enoch's, Glasgow, Victoria Station, Nottingham, Fenchurch Street, and Liverpool Street, London. These developments were carried out with speed and verve. What is different now is not only that the social impact of these developments has become politically more important – though it has – but that the *delays in implementation have become far greater*. Amazing numbers of people have to have a say in the processes (even excluding the general public!) and this clogs the machine.

Local Action

There are four possible kinds of local action, each one of which is described in the following chapters, and they are in brief:

(a) To brighten up a blighted area which is not about to be immediately redeveloped so that at least it makes the locality tolerable to live in.

(b) To devise short-term uses for blighted areas which will not take too much money or time, and could be demolished when the development occurs.

(c) Because so much blight is caused by Council inaction, inability, or delay, local people and groups should consider doing some of the Council's work themselves.

(d) The longer term view of (c) is that local groups could look forward to taking over permanently some of the Council work in their own area.

Occupying the Land

The very fact that there are hundreds of thousands of acres of land lying in one form of dereliction or another provides an opportunity for local groups and communities to start the process of reviving their own area. It should not normally be difficult to negotiate permission for temporary use with the owner of a piece of land. Land ownership details, particularly for small patches, can be difficult to trace, but either the local Council's planning department, or the valuation rolls (which should be available either at the Council's offices or in the library) should provide the information. In most city centres, it is likely that the land is owned by the Council.

Most Councils are obsessed with *power*, and they will not respond if they consider that they will lose the power over the land they own. For this reason, they are more likely to be persuaded to let the land be occupied under a formal lease, than either to part with a freehold, or to tolerate an occupation. Be warned: even in these enlightened days nobody should underestimate the vindictiveness of an antagonised Council. In London recently, one Council had a load of rubbish dumped on an adventure playground which was occupying derelict Council-owned land.

Occupying land without permission constitutes trespass, and if the owner can prove damage, he may take civil action. However, in many cases the owner may be far away from his land or may not even know that he does own it; and, if the site is small, he is unlikely to take offence at its cultivation. In most of the cases which are discussed later in this book, permission to use the land has been a relatively small problem, except when the land is owned by one of the few notorious Councils who will permit nobody to touch Council land except itself – even if the said Council won't act itself.

The normal procedure for acquiring the use of unoccupied land is that the land-owner will issue a lease, which he sees as a technical defence against the users claiming permanent squatters' rights in 12 years' time. Such leases also make the transactions look formal and seem less like charity (an example is given in the next chapter). When the Tolmers Village Association in London took over and subsequently negotiated the land for their community garden, the owners not only gave them a lease at £1 per annum, but also donated £25 towards paint and seats.[1] Thus some private owners can be persuaded that a good, community-based use of previously derelict land is good publicity for them.

Time-scale of Investment

It is sensible to take a realistic view of the length of time the land will be available when considering how much money to spend. Here is a suggested financial time-scale:

(a) *Temporary use of the land:* up to two years, requiring little financial outlay.
(b) *Semi-permanent use of the land:* a range of, say, three to five years; it would be worthwhile erecting temporary buildings which could be removed and perhaps re-erected elsewhere.
(c) *Indefinite use of the land:* a substantial financial investment is possible; and a local community doing this work could consider building its own housing and community facilities.

This kind of estimate can have many advantages, particularly when negotiating with the Council or the land-owner. It helps to give them a clear idea of what is being proposed for their land and over what period. Also, local Councils may issue temporary licences for some kinds of structures for which it would be unlikely to give a permanent permit.

If a clear and realistic assessment is not made at the beginning, a great deal of labour could be wasted on land which would only be available for a few months. Volunteer effort is too precious a resource to be used in a spendthrift way.

Time has a knack of making temporary projects permanent (as the continued existence of the post-war prefabs shows), and so although some of the low investment projects are intended to last for only a short time it is a good idea to make them to such a high standard that they can survive for a long time if this becomes possible.

The common themes that run through the following case studies are: (*a*) occupying the land; (*b*) the investment required, seen in terms of time, volunteer labour and finance; (*c*) how negotiations were carried out; and (*d*) what professional advice was required. The problems raised by these questions are discussed in Chapter 11, where changes to current procedures or legislation are considered.

Reference
1. *Community Action* magazine. Issue 14.

Of interest
Empty Property – a guide to local groups (Shelter, 30p).
Another Empty Home (Shelter report, 40p).

4 · THE GREENING OF
THE CITY

No matter what administrative reforms could be devised to speed the process of development, there will always be some land which is not required for immediate use; and as long as it is there it will attract vandalism and litter. There is also a further category of blight which might be called *no man's land* – it consists of small stretches and parcels of land which have been long neglected and the ownership is often unclear. This can vary from neglected roadside verges, and odd patches which seem to belong to no one; to railway cuttings and embankments which belong to British Rail but are usually abandoned; to over-wide pavements (perhaps the relics of an ancient but now abandoned road widening proposal); land left over after a new development which is often screened by chicken-wire or fencing; useless lengths of new or widened roads, or dual carriageways which will not be completed (such as Franciscan Way in Ipswich, Barker Gate in Nottingham, or the new stretch of road in the Aylesbury area, Walworth, London); and finally, the ground-level areas in many council estates which is often dismally restricted to tarmac or 'municipal carpet' (grass), which the tenants are prevented from making more productive or attractive.

Why Grow Flowers?

One of the quickest ways to make an area pleasant (if even for only a short time) is by the cultivation of flowers and vegetables. If a few well-cared-for and lush window boxes can make a substantial difference to the atmosphere of a street, how much greater an improvement will be caused by the cultivation of a derelict site? Land used for growing flowers or vegetables will be more pleasant to live near than land lying unused, and it will look cared for, thus perhaps deterring vandalism. The air will carry the scents of flowers and vegetables which can be very pleasant; and there will be a greater variety of colours than before, changing with the seasons (town dwellers need reminding sometimes that there are such things as seasons). The hard lines of streets and buildings can be softened with climbing flowers, creepers and ivies – and few sights are more beautiful than a building covered in virginia creeper which is turning red and gold with the autumn. Plants and flowers also attract animals, birds and insects. All in all, increased cultivation throughout towns and cities could produce a more balanced natural life than is provided by the arid environment of tarmac, brick and concrete.

...HOME iS A NICE IDEA...

Economics of Cultivation

The Friends of the Earth point out that Britain spends over £3,000 million per annum on imported food but allows some 75,000 acres of arable land to be lost to agriculture each year. This is very bad husbandry, particularly while development continues to eat into the available agricultural land, and there would be no shortage of willing volunteers to carry out the cultivation of derelict land. At least 57,000 people in Britain are registered on allotment waiting lists; and since some authorities have closed their lists, and others do not keep waiting lists at all, it is possible that the actual number of those willing to garden is far higher. There may also be many more people who might not be prepared to take on an allotment, some distance from their home, but who would be prepared to help produce a communal garden on a nearby derelict site. Allotments are governed by law, and can range up to a size of 40 poles – whatever they may be! (1 pole $= 5\frac{1}{2}$ yds); they require a formal lease from the Council, and are rarely conveniently placed, being usually relegated to a remote and fairly inaccessible spot; and for many people they still have psychological connections with the Depression. If, on the other hand, local communities or groups combined to buy their own gardening tools, then it would require far less dedication merely to go out and dig up that derelict spot around the corner.

For those prepared to dig, the economic return will match the care with which the land is planted. A 300 sq. yd patch could save up to £130 per annum in fresh vegetables in return for 3 hours' digging per week.[1]

It was no accident that the builders of mediaeval cities always left enough space for gardens and orchards within the encircling walls since, during a time of siege, home-grown food could prove essential to a city's survival. The same philosophy during the last war led to the 'Dig for Victory' campaign in which gardens, allotments, verges and bits of parks were used for growing food. It could be argued that Britain is currently in the face of economic siege, in which case the financial arguments for cultivation would be even stronger than the amenity arguments. Was it charity or

The Kentish Town Fun Art Farm. The community workshop is in the centre, and cows and goats are kept in the sheds on the left.

foresight that led Islington Council to provide a fruit tree in each garden on a new housing estate two years ago?

City Farms

In a typical area of neglect, alongside the railways of London's Kentish Town, the Inter-Action Fun Art Farm can be found. It may well be the forerunner of city farms in other towns and cities. The farm was founded by an organisation called the Neighbourhood Use of Buildings and Space (NUBS), a branch of the Inter-Action advisory service concerned with self-help, and according to their brochure:

'The crux of NUBS is that voluntary self help groups are cheaper, quicker, less bureaucratic and more democratic than statutorily implemented projects. Voluntary projects will incur little or no rejection (including vandalism) from the surrounding community.'

The land for the Fun Art Farm was obtained from British Rail which owns much similar property, often jammed between rail-

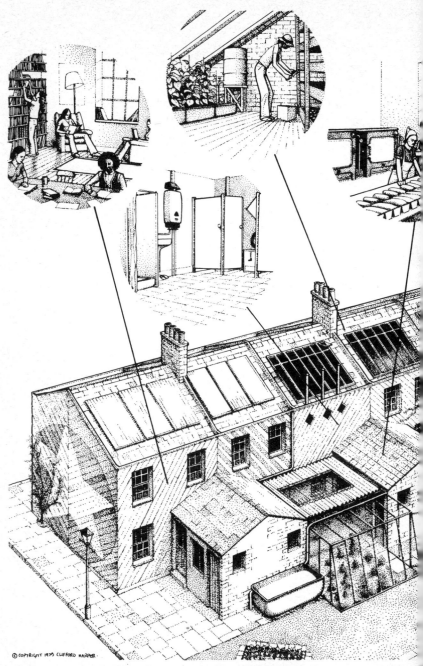

1: AUTONOMOUS TER

ACE

THIS WAS DRAWN BY CLIFFORD HARPER.

way lines and deprived housing areas built following the construction of the railway in the nineteenth century. BR judged that there was virtually no market value for the land and consequently the city farm pays a rent of only £1 per week. Negotiations were interesting, and Ed Berman, a director of NUBS and founder of Inter-Action, maintains that BR listened to sweet reason. One of the conversations seems to have gone as follows:

BR   We are interested but we are worried about security, people getting onto the lines and so on.
Berman Don't you have some lines running alongside house gardens?
BR   Yes.
Berman So what do you do about security there?
BR   Require an 8 ft high fence.
Berman OK, we'll erect an 8 ft high fence around our farm.

The negotiations were so successful that British Rail have now recommended its regions to consider (sympathetically) applications for other city farms on similar sites, and Inter-Action has a grant of £15,000 from the DoE to carry on developing the idea.

Berman stresses that not all age groups are interested in the same activities, and energetic children are not as likely to be interested in allotments and cultivation as the middle aged. Consequently the Fun Art Farm provides activities for each age group: for the old people there is a shared communal garden and a club house; for the middle aged there are allotments and the workshop (though it is used by all ages); and for the kids there are stables, a riding school, a tack room, and a farm rearing cows, pigs, goats, hens and rabbits. It sounds almost Arcadian, and indeed the Farm is a splendid place, but it must be remembered that the people working on this project, as with the others described in this book are in the front line against the violence, aggression, decay and dereliction prevalent in these areas. It is a most significant achievement to deflect any of this aggression, and Berman would like to do research based on the Farm experience into the effect of animals on human beings. For example, do large animals which can hurt and yet are vulnerable and need to be fed and looked after, create a sense of responsibility in kids?

The following scale of investment has been worked out for city farms:

The Indoor Riding School at the Kentish Town Farm.

(*a*) A labour-intensive farm with little or no capital, and no full-time staff, run entirely by local people who wish to improve their territory. This would involve perhaps, some cultivation, re-using a derelict building or two, and keeping a few animals.

(*b*) More investment – more hens for instance, and perhaps letting the kids set up a local egg-selling business, using the money gained to buy things for the farm.

(*c*) Acquiring larger animals – goats, pigs and bullocks – some of which can be bought for as little as £1 each when small, and then resold when fattened at a price which covers the cost of the feed. During the interim the kids would have learned how to look after the animals properly.

(*d*) Buying specialised animals such as horses, thus providing another opportunity for the kids – selling manure for local window boxes.

(*e*) Finally, intensive capital investment; full-time staff and valuable animals and equipment. The keeping of animals should pay for itself, either through the sales of eggs, milk or manure, or through charging for visiting school parties or for riding lessons.

According to Berman, the caretakers of the surrounding estates say that vandalism has plummeted since the opening of this City Farm. That in itself is surely recommendation enough.

Surrey Docks Farm

Hilary Peters, co-organiser of the Surrey Docks Farm with Ken Bushell, is particularly interested in the effect of animals on children:

'Although Surrey Docks has kestrels, rabbits and pigeons, our main predators are human. Total unfamiliarity with the land has made local children intensely curious and sometimes violent in their attitudes towards animals. . . . Most of the children we meet have no idea of where food comes from. They are frightened of animals and this fear is expressed either in violence or in running away. If we can show the local kids that animals leading a reasonably natural life can produce enough for their own needs and ours as well, that waste land can be used to produce vegetables and waste food recycled to produce milk and eggs, it removes a great fear of unknown horrors.'[2]

Surrey Docks Farm is located on derelict Port of London Authority land scheduled for redevelopment in the near future, and regards itself as mainly educational, providing a place where children can see goats being milked and fed, watch cheese-making, bee-keeping, and look after hens and donkeys. Peters and Bushell are hoping to be able to develop the poultry club to include ducks, and if that produces a surplus of eggs to sell, they might begin a delivery round with a horse and cart which, with all the ancillary activities to do with horses, could provide the children with a lot more to do. Much of the feed for the animals is donated from scraps either by local residents or by local shops, in return for which eggs and milk are given to the donors.

According to Ed Berman the essential difference between the Surrey Docks venture and the Kentish Town Fun Art Farm is that the Surrey Docks Farm was not born out of a local desire to do

Brick Windmill, built in two weeks as an exhibit for the Habitat Festival in the Surrey Docks, and now used to pump water to allotments in the docks. It was designed by Bryn Bird on a similar basis as Cretan windmills, but may fall foul of the planning authorities!

something, but out of a desire by non-locals to prove an ecological point of view. Yet it is possible that little use would ever have been made of the derelict areas of Surrey Docks (ironically, before the docks were built, the land was renowned through Britain for fine asparagus, onions and other market garden produce) had not Ken Bushell and Hilary Peters started the Farm. There is room for both approaches.

Both of these schemes *work*, and provide facilities which officialdom does not; indeed the nearest that officialdom seems to get to such a project is either by simply allowing it to happen (by lending or renting the land) or by producing something like the Lambeth Country Show. This country show, held in Brockwell Park, South London, was a brave attempt to bring the country to the town, with cows and pigs, bee-keeping, shire horses, the army and show jumping, all to be seen for two days, during which the atmosphere was genuinely semi-bucolic. However, it was noticed that few blacks visited the show even though it was located in a predominantly black area; in other words, the local people were not really involved. It was the first time I had seen Brockwell Park used to such effect, and I would have thought that a permanent city farm project in one corner of the park could be in keeping with the general aims of the Parks Department (open space and recreation) and provide something more besides.

Flowering the City

Since gardens are usually hidden away behind houses, and allotments are frequently situated in out-of-the-way areas, the cultivation of no man's land is likely to have a great visual impact on the street. It requires little effort to buy clematis, honeysuckle, climbing roses, or indeed any of the 80-odd varieties of ivy which range in colour from green, to gold or lemon leaves, and plant them at the foot of buildings. Obviously some care needs to be taken if the plant is not to die and the money be wasted, but provided it has a wee bit of soil, and a suitable orientation (for some do not like hot areas) these climbers soon develop lives of their own, attracting birds to nest in them, and some such as quince, produce a good fruit into the bargain.

No man's land, in this case owned by the local council. What a difference would be made to the street by some flowers, or vegetables or even grass.

The cultivation of small pieces of no man's land is a field for minor victories. Take this recent example from Camberwell, London:

A group of residents decided to cultivate the strip of land between the drives of their houses and the pavement; it contains a splendid avenue of horse chestnuts, but the areas surrounding the trees consisted of beaten earth, broken glass and a general mess. The reason for tackling this little strip was two-fold: firstly it looked depressing, and secondly it was hoped that other households would follow suit so that these strips of earth all up the street would soon be cultivated, making an improvement to the area generally. The land had been abandoned for so long that the earth had become packed hard, and people had become used to walking across it. Hard crusts of stones, broken milk bottles, iron, litter and bricks had formed through which the rain had obviously not percolated for years. Moving the rubbish even from this tiny site was quite a job, and beneath it the earth was found to have broken into crisp lumps attached to stones – which only separated from each other after heavy water saturation. However, months afterwards, worms kept bringing to the surface more rubble and glass of which there seemed to be an inexhaustible store beneath. The dry summer kept the earth arid, and consequently only flowers like begonias and busy lizzies survived. Local dogs (and their owners) are the greatest enemy and both pepper and anti-dog pills have proved inadequate; yet, even if the land were acquired for a development tomorrow, this six months of having flowers growing on it has provided a morale boost to the area. Unfortunately no other occupiers have followed suit to cultivate the bit of land in front of their houses (in this case most belonging to the Council) – a great opportunity wasted.

Some people feel apprehensive about digging up Council land even for praiseworthy aims, and I was assured by one amenity society that if tenants planted anything they could be sure that

The timescale of cultivation.

Typical inter-war London housing estate, with neglected and sterile ground areas.

the Council would come to dig it up. Many Council estates have poor grounds; some which were constructed in the 'twenties and 'thirties had their buildings neatly arranged round courtyards – but the courtyard areas belong to no one in particular. In some instances, no doorways open directly on to them so the tenants have to walk round the entire building to reach them. People digging, planting flowers or vegetables with others watching them or helping would do more to foster a community spirit than bleak courtyards.

Tree Planting

Permission for tree planting beside the highway usually has to be obtained from the Council's surveyor, and any group may plant trees if it wishes to improve its area. The same care should be taken over the choice of trees for a particular location as over the choice of vegetables or creepers. Groups must be prepared for a refusal from the Council on the grounds that the tree will damage underground services (sewage, water, gas and electricity pipes), but this answer can be the result of ignorance of the effect of the various types of trees and of the actual location of these under-pavement pipes. Consequently, some people have found that it is easier to locate the correct spot and plant the tree before getting permission, rather than to follow the more normal procedures. No complaints have yet been received.

Gardens and Allotments

Many people are either temperamentally unwilling or physically incapable of cultivating their own gardens, with the result that many gardens are neglected. The cause might be something quite simple and blameless such as the householder suffering a slipped disc; or it could be that the lettings policy of the local Council does not take into account the interests of a prospective tenant, in which case many properties with fine gardens are let to those who have no interest in maintaining them. The Friends of the Earth 'Crops and Shares'[3] scheme is intended to 'put those people who have under-used gardens which they would like to see cultivated, into contact with people wanting land to grow food'. Some twenty out of the FoE's 140 British groups are already operating such schemes one of which, in Horsham, has been running for two years without trouble. Both gardener and garden-owner share the produce according to the agreement drawn up between them, and the FoE consider that great public benefit could be achieved if local Councils would promote such sharing in their own districts, as some London Boroughs are now doing.

Many Councils regard allotments as a burden and are unwilling to devote more land or money to them. The use, size, title and lease of allotments are all laid down in a variety of Acts of Parliament and it is for this reason that the less precise 'communal gardens' may be more acceptable to Councils than the proposal to convert a derelict site in formal allotments. During the affluent 'fifties and 'sixties, the demand for allotments fell, but times have changed, and the current investment by Councils in allotments as compared to other activities shows that many have not yet caught up with the change of attitude evidenced by the lengthening allotment waiting lists. The excellent FoE Allotment Manual for Newcastle[4] discloses that in 1975 the Council was prepared to spend only £1,640 on its 1,509 allotments – a ratio of just over £1 per allotment – whereas it was proposed to spend £11,600 on the Westerhope Golf Course which has only 750 members – a ratio of about £15 per member. Allotments provide both cultivation and recreation, whereas golf courses provide simply recreation.

Waterloo: Derelict Site into Allotment

In order to give a specific focus to their 1974 allotments campaign, the Friends of the Earth chose a site in London to cultivate 'pour encourager les autres'. The aim of the campaign was to 'highlight the fact that vast acreages of land were standing idle in most areas of the UK and to promote the short-term use of that land until such time as development commences'. The site chosen was prominent, nearly opposite the Old Vic Theatre just along the road from the Young Vic, and down the road from Waterloo Station. The site had been purchased some 20 years before by the London County Council for housing, but no action had been taken. It supported a variety of wild life including apple, plum and peach trees which had been sown by the casual discarding of stones and pips by passers-by.

Negotiations were carried out, initially with the Greater London Council's Planning Department, then with its Director General's office, and eventually with a host of other departments. The FoE went to the GLC on a 'Why don't you co-operate and help us?' basis to which they agreed; the FoE then went as far as to draw up a draft occupancy agreement which runs as follows:

'FoE hereby formally requests the GLC to give its permission for members of FoE and members of the local community to use the land available at the side of The Cut, London SE1 for the purposes of growing food. We further request that the GLC makes available the necessary funds to enable the aforesaid organisation and individuals to purchase equipment with which to facilitate the efficient running of the site and growing of food. We undertake to vacate the site when the owners can give

Allotment on previously derelict ground in London.

assurances that the development of the site will commence within 6 months of the serving of a notice to quit.'[5]

Unfortunately, all did not go smoothly:

'Sadly (the GLC's) procrastination meant that we were left with no alternative but to occupy the site without their permission, if the campaign was to meet the deadline. After initial fury from the GLC at our action, they succumbed to rational persuasion and have been offering other sites in London to FoE groups for the same short term purposes.'[6]

Preparing the site was difficult because a house at the end had been demolished and its bricks spread liberally over the entire area. They were subsequently used for footpaths and retaining walls.

'The order of the day was maximum improvisation and sensible use of resources to hand. Any soil, given the right treatment, will become suitable for growing food and since part of the original soil was clay based, we turned it so that it could be broken down by frost. The rest of the soil was good enough to be used immediately once the rubble was cleared away.'

At the moment, thirteen allotments and gardens of various

shapes and sizes exist on what used to be an 'alcoholics' crash pad'; and the fertile soil had already produced swedes, potatoes, tomatoes, melons, purple sprouting broccoli, sprouts, carrots, lettuce, spinach, beetroot, radishes, leeks, parsnips, and artichokes. Vandalism has 'been kept to a mimimum by the kindness of bus inspectors who throw off anybody they do not recognise, and being on good terms with the bus people has been necessary for survival' (because access is through bus property).

'The good thing about this plot is that it is not just a bunch of young freaks who will lose interest after a year. Most of the people are middle aged and *local*.'[7]

The FoE consider that the political effect of the allotments campaign has been encouraging in view of the fact that some local authorities have become responsive to requests for short-term use of derelict land. Very detailed information on allotments, leases, negotiations, handling the press and on vegetable growing are contained in the FoE's allotment campaign manual.[5] One word of caution, however, is that there is no such thing as 'instant cultivation'. The success of the Waterloo allotment depended on 'being prepared to see the campaign through from start to finish, and being fully aware that there is a lot of back-breaking work to be put into it. It is essential that all legal channels be investigated before a takeover (which is strictly an illegal act) can be contemplated.'[6] This example has been chosen to illustrate some of the problems encountered, and there are already many similar projects throughout the United Kingdom. Even in its own small area, the Covent Garden Community has managed to use a number of sites for communal gardening.

Experimentation

The ability to use derelict land seems to free the users from the normal constraints and restricted attitudes which prevail when developing more central, high-profit land. It is on derelict or unused land that can be seen many of the more interesting communal, ecological, alternative technology or self-help experiments. Although ecological experiments cannot strictly be classed as 'cultivation' the aim to provide a more balanced and natural life is similar. The 'Habitat' venture, for example, which lasted for a week in the Surrey Docks, coinciding with the United Nations Vancouver Habitat Conference, included building windmills, erecting solar shields, digging allotments, and endless teach-ins. There was little permanent construction save the

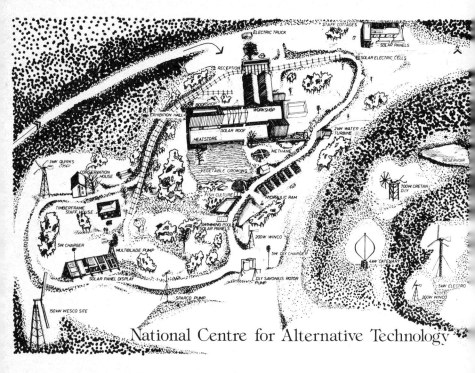

National Centre for Alternative Technology

windmill which now pumps water from a nearby lagoon to the allotments, but the fact that people could be watched making these artifacts rendered the whole subject slightly less cranky than it might otherwise have been.

Of greater permanence is the National Centre for Alternative Technology – located in the disused Llwyngwern slate quarry at Pantperthog, near Machynlleth, mid-Wales. Over the last three years this centre has been developing new methods of producing energy and visitors can see not only the recycling of rubbish to produce methane, but also solar collectors, electric panels, windmills, aerogenerators, fish farming, electric transport, organic vegetable farming, and rainwater harnessed through a reservoir to produce power. The Wates Foundation has contributed and completed a large house specially designed for exceptionally low-energy consumption – with most of the energy being produced by the wind – knowing that the entire subject of low-energy technology has progressed well beyond the flat-earthers. Wates estimate that the house costs about £2,000 more than normal house but that it should save some 85 per cent on fuel bills. The house's elegant appearance disproves the accusation that 'ecological' houses necessarily look messy or occupy too much land. These voluntary efforts should be compared to the fact that the Government find it easy to spend some £400 million on developing potentially lethal nuclear reactors.

Conclusion

There is plenty of land lying waiting to be used, the occupation of it should prove no problem, and the only real obstacle to comprehensive action is the psychological stumbling block of being prepared to cultivate land that is not *yours*. The best way to resolve this is to begin digging. Exhortations about careful planning and planting were aimed at the purist; plants and vegetables survive perfectly well in the wild, so that all that really needs to be done is to prepare the soil to receive them.

References
1. *The Sunday Times*, 21 March 1976.
2. ILEA *Contact*, 2 May 1976.
3. *Crops and Shares*. Friends of the Earth, 9 Poland Street, London W1.
4. *Gaining Ground*. FoE Newcastle Report, 45p.
5. *FoE Allotments Campaign Manual* – and excellent source of information – 45p from the above address.
6. Letter from Pete Wilkinson to Charles McKean, 26 May 1976.
7. Letter from Rob Arber to Charles McKean, 31 May 1976.

Books worth reading

There are endless books on gardening, probably all equally good. Some simple publications which can be personally recommended are:

Mr Smith's Vegetable Garden, BBC, 60p.

Garden Nature Reserve, published by Watch Advisory Centre for Education, 32 Trumpington Street, Cambridge, £1.00.

NUBS brochure, 14 Talacre Road, London NW5.

Dig For Survival (Laurence Hills, Henry Doubleday Research Association, 20 Convent Lane, Bocking, Braintree, Essex, price 5p).

The Back Yard Dairy Book by Len Street and Andrew Singer, Prism Press, £1.00.

5 · INEXPENSIVE AND TEMPORARY IMPROVEMENTS

The process of urban decay is very demoralising for people who have to live with it; and this chapter deals with relatively inexpensive projects which can be undertaken to restore or maintain a community's self-confidence. Only once this has been achieved is it likely that positive action can be taken towards making some more permanent improvements. Some people might claim that such activities are merely 'tarting up' a district, a cosmetic activity making no contribution to solving the urban or social problems of today. Perhaps they don't; but they certainly make life very much more agreeable for the local people while they are waiting for such critics to produce the brave new world.

Clean-up Campaigns

Clean-up campaigns in many different guises – such as '20 Ideas for Bristol' or 'Face-lift Glasgow' – have been used for some years as an effective way of channelling public enthusiasm into practical work. In theory, maintaining the environment to a reasonable standard is the duty of the local authority, and conversely its neglect is one of the most obvious symptoms of local authority breakdown. Evidence of this is widespread, but a good example can be seen in a new Lambeth Council housing scheme which has spray-paint graffiti on some of its doors; not an unusual event, were it not for the fact that directly across the road from this estate is the Lambeth Works Department. If the administrative system was functioning properly, the men in the Works Department should have popped across the road to have scrubbed the graffiti from their own buildings; or if the social system had worked, the tenants should have scrubbed it off themselves. Obviously, unless local groups undertake some of this clean-up work, it will probably not get done at all.

The range of local campaigns undertaken in recent years is vast, ranging from clearing river banks, monitoring pollution, clearing up Highgate Cemetery and restoring it from the ravages of neglect and vandals, organising school groups to paint over graffiti on local walls, co-ordinating over 20 youth groups and school groups as part of the major 'Heritage over the Wensum' project in Norwich, right down to a recent application by the Oswaldtwistle Civic Society for 11 schemes for tidying up derelict areas in the town to be carried out under the job creation programme. These included clearing streams, tidying up derelict land, tidying back streets, rubbish-filled lanes and beauty spots, improving fencing of rural roads, improving street nameplates, and rebuilding dry stone walls. Some local communities have organised their own litter bins, and one group in Peckham which had become dissatisfied with the Council's rubbish collection, organised its own skip to pick up rubbish and take it away.

The Value of Paint

We have become too used to a sub-standard, grimy and cheap environment. We no longer question why the netting which encloses playgrounds, railway lines, football pitches, tennis courts and the like must always be grey, black or rusty. The effort involved in painting such enclosures orange or any other bright colour would be little compared to the resulting benefits. Looking at other rusting fences, railings, unused walls, the normal dull, grey lamp standards, or even minor detail like water hydrants and kerbstones, one might almost conclude that there was a conspiracy to ensure that modern environments were predominantly grey. The Greater London Council has itself shown the extent to which paint can transform an environment by painting the main river bridges over the Thames in a variety of colours.

The electricity transformer box in Sunnyside, Wimbledon, restored to something of its former glory by local people.

The lovely deep red, gold and black colours of Lambeth Bridge naturally match the Tudor bricks of Lambeth Palace, but who would ever have thought that the dull black, monstrously designed, Hungerford Bridge which runs between the Royal Festival Hall and Charing Cross could have been so transformed by the skilful use of red?

It is up to local enthusiasts to decide what they wish to do, and a splendid example of initiative was recently shown in Wimbledon, where a fine mid-Victorian electricity transformer chamber box was transmogrified out of the normal LEB flaking green paint into something magnificent, decorated in gold and white on a black background.

Murals

There is nothing new in using paint to decorate buildings, although it has been more frequent in Mediterranean countries than in Britain. If one looks at certain famous tourist spots such as Portofino (Italy) one will realise that those splendid tenements facing the port (which have been photographed by millions of admiring tourists) are in fact really plain tall tenements. Their attraction lies in their beautiful paintings; paintings which create the illusion of something which is not there: above each window is a beautifully scrolled pediment, beneath each window are details of stones, and the whole ensemble creates the illusion of palatial buildings. They create interest where none exists, and this principle could be applied for example to decorating some of our more featureless tower blocks (how would you decide which tower blocks were more featureless than others?), and to gable ends – which are so prominent in derelict areas, or to walls. The essential difference between this type of painting and the painting which one can see, for example, in Camden Town on the railway bridge, is that murals create an illusion, as opposed to merely brightening up something that would otherwise look tatty.

Modern mural painting is being developed to a high degree in the USA, and some American examples are beautiful in their precision and effect – particularly in the way they manage to

Mural painting at the base of a dreary tower block in Deptford. Its bright colours are a considerable advance on damp-stained concrete.

transform the gable walls of buildings into a distant landscape, so that the building itself becomes virtually invisible. There are examples in London – and the Scottish Arts Council recently commissioned three artists to do full-size murals on gable walls in Partick, Glasgow.

A recently published murals kit by Michael Norton[1] describes in detail some of the procedures for painting a mural. For example, it is advisable to choose north-facing walls, so that the colours do not fade in the sun; and the condition of the wall must be reasonable if the mural is to stick. In murals, perhaps more than in any other type of activity, the final appearance is important. There is a strong belief that freedom of expression should be permitted – particularly to children – and that the result will *ipso facto* be good. However, common sense will show that in any area which is suffering from decay and dereliction a wall which is scrappily painted will not look that much different from its neighbouring walls covered in graffiti. If the aim of raising the morale of the neighbourhood is to be achieved, then some quality in a mural is going to be essential.

Transient Activities

Once sites have been cleared and tidied, there are many valuable uses which could take place on them, such as local markets, fairs, concerts, open air plays, public meeting places (perhaps the reintroduction of the concept of the old Roman Forum?), simple sitting-out parks or adventure playgrounds. In other words some sites could perform the same function for a local community as the old village green. However, if travelling people, fairs, orators or markets are to be attracted then the appearance of these sites becomes important; if they look tatty, visitors will not come. For example, a site in central Greenwich which had been derelict for many years has been used at weekends for a small successful jumble market. However, before the market arrived the site was cleared and covered with some gravel. It was all that was required, but it made all the difference.

Community Festivals

Few things are so effective in the restoration of an area's morale, as the organisation of a community festival or fair, especially if they also perform the valuable function of fund-raising. Festivals can bring together people who have lived in the same locality for many years who have never met each other, such as the festival held in Meard Street, Soho in 1975, organised by Stephen Fry.

'It's time we all began to realise that Soho is a beautiful place to live, not just a playground for second-rate drunks, visiting football crowds and noisy club owning bums who think it's their right to disturb the streets all night.'[2]

A much more radical festival was that held by the Save Piccadilly campaign in 1972 (the organisers included Ed Berman and Michael Norton) which consisted of an entire weekend's programme of events designed to encourage locals, passers-by and

A spectacular example of a mural which creates an illusion, here painted on a gable end in Floyd Road, Charlton. This was painted by the Greenwich murals workshop and local residents, and was paid for with help from the Council and the Greater London Arts Association.

tourists taking an interest in the future of Piccadilly Circus. The tactics used by the Save Piccadilly campaign revolutionised attitudes towards public participation and planning.

The 1975 Soho Festival, which was held in the graveyard of St Anne's Church, gives some idea of what is involved in organising a community festival. It took a very long time to organise and the aim was to make a profit for use by the Soho Society. The initial outlay was almost £800, which went to hiring the public address system, printing teeshirts, programmes, balloons, and in organising the various artists to take part. Many Soho restaurants set up stalls in the churchyard and on the site of the ruined church nave and Jeff Long formed the Soho Festival Orchestra for the occasion. The affair had a vivid cosmopolitan flavour. There was a net profit of £600 which met the organisers' target.

Adventure Playgrounds

Adventure playgrounds are frequently seized upon as a form of activity to be placed on an empty site which will benefit local kids. By their nature, they will not necessarily look nice and are likely to attract a certain amount of mess, and it is ironic that many of the poorer families for whose kids these playgrounds were developed oppose them on the grounds of dirt, noise, and general scruffiness. Such, for example, was the initial reaction to the Soho adventure playground. There are other problems. In many cases, adventure playgrounds are organised by the active mothers of children; and what has sadly proved to be a common occurrence is that these children have been overwhelmed by the tougher kids who have been attracted into the playground. This is possibly because some of the play leaders available at playgrounds do not have sufficient creativity or personal authority to control the tougher kids or to divert youthful energy into positive action. Many adventure playgrounds have been burned down, and where the committee's mothers find that the playground is overrun by the tougher kids, they withdraw their support and the playground closes.

This process is almost inevitable if a single function – such as an adventure playground – is located in a deprived area, for it acts

A new wall, paid for by the residents of the houses on the left and designed in such a way that it looks as though it could have been there for centuries. An example of local initiative.

like a honey-pot attracting people of a certain age in highly concentrated numbers. The result is always likely to be trouble. It may well be that the NUBS city farms to which people of all ages are attracted for various activities could provide a better solution.

A Wall

Small but highly significant improvements to an area can be made by a group of householders or occupiers clubbing together for that purpose. A recent, unspectacular, example of this has occurred in Camberwell where a new wall and fence, in traditional style, has been erected to replace the old fence which was cut down during the last war to provide armaments. This new wall, nicely designed, rendered and painted in keeping with the colour of the houses, well suits its historic environment both in scale and in the way it restores a sense of space to the street. Few people would realise that it had been built for barely six months instead of 150 years.

Temporary Uses of Buildings

Some groups have taken over and repaired buildings for temporary uses; local residents in the Raleigh Street clearance areas of Nottingham have taken over a derelict shop to provide a supervised play centre for young children.[3] The residents have cleaned, redecorated, rewired, replastered, replumbed the house and have replaced several broken windows. The house was derelict because it was in a clearance area, and the owner's only concern was lest this takeover might affect the compensation the Council would offer after a compulsory purchase order was complete. Which is unlikely. A similar project is proposed in the Louvaine Road area, Wandsworth, where local groups have applied for Urban Aid grants to convert a disused Victorian church into a day nursery and a community centre, these uses being chosen after a questionnaire which had been circulated to all local people. In Rotherhithe, an investigation has been carried out into whether an old air raid shelter could be converted into a launderette and social centre in a remote and rather deprived housing estate; and in Covent Garden, the local community has converted a warehouse into a community centre – including a club room, facilities for giving evening classes, press conferences, lectures and a crèche. Oxfam and Shelter shops and those of other charities tend to occupy empty and short-life property to excellent effect.

Ideas Exhibitions

Few people are able to visualise what something would be like without seeing a drawing or model of it, and it is for that reason that ideas exhibitions are so important. Exhibitions such as the '20 Ideas for Bristol' exhibition can provoke both the authorities and local communities into taking positive action to improve the environment. Models also can be a help. When Keith Cheng was trying to raise support for his proposed water garden in Covent Garden (see next section but two) he found it necessary to build a model so that he could show people what he was planning to do. Ideas exhibitions, models, or the helping of local people by skilled artists and illustrators to demonstrate what alternatives to any proposed development there could be are invaluable in stimulating local initiative. The ARAU group in Brussels have been carrying out a guerilla campaign against the city council for the last few years by producing and illustrating alternative proposals for most of the major new developments in the centre of Brussels, thus giving the citizens of Brussels the first opportunity they have ever had of choosing between two alternatives.

Ideas Competitions

The holding of ideas competitions is a good method both of focusing attention on a given area and stimulating a variety of proposed solutions to the problems. A recent example is the Victoria Square Competition, Birmingham, supported by the local architects, the Civic Society, the local newspaper and the Council.[4] The Square was once the town's major square but had become neglected. The winner proposes to make the Square more noticeable by the creation of a large flight of steps, the planting of avenues of trees, and the creation of a sculpture with curved reflecting mirrors. The promoters are delighted with the result, with the variety of ideas they received, and also with the intense interest expressed by ordinary people. A similar ideas competition was held by the North East Thames Society of Architects in 1975 in which competitors were asked to suggest proposals for the neglected (left-over) area of Cassland Road, Hackney. The winner proposed such unspectacular solutions as re-using an empty building, closing a street, building a few houses in the gaps, and doing some planting. The winner (Guy Gervis) made these low-key proposals because they could all be achieved.

Art into Landscape

One of the more stimulating projects so far held in the field of temporary land use was the 1974 Arts Council competition entitled 'Art into Landscape', which was launched with the help of the RIBA and the Institute of Landscape Architects. The idea came from Hubert Dalwood, a sculptor and chairman of the Serpentine Committee in London:

'To do what we must do with our world, we must use our imaginations. It is a simple (and as complex) as that, and that is what this exhibition is about. Imagination is not the prerogative of any professional age group and so the competition was left open to anyone, artist, layman or child, who cared about his environment. Some of the schemes are impractical and even grandiose, some are humble and relate to the small places that an artist (what else should I call him?) knows and cares about. Together they demonstrate that imagination is more important than any particular expertise.'

Norbert Lynton, director of exhibitions for the Arts Council, says in his introduction to the catalogue:

'What ideas have people got for turning open spaces that might be messy and uninviting into places that one might enjoy and relax in? A lot of our environment is designed by specially trained people; a lot just happens; a lot was not meant to get into the state it has but money or time or interest has run out.'[5]

Entries for this competition included a proposal for growing grass on the sides of multi-storey buildings, the re-use of a neglected area beneath railway arches, using the Old Kent Road flyover as a roller skating ramp on Sundays, and the suggestion that there should be a farm in the middle of Kensington Gardens. The entries were primarily visual and herein lies the real value. It is a pity that the exhibition was largely organised by intellectuals, entered by intellectuals and visited by intellectuals. The fantastic visual skills which are obviously available throughout the country should be made more available at a local level for local people to take the opportunity of improving their own environment locally.

Japanese Water Garden

Once a site has been taken over for community use, it is not enough merely to scatter a bit of gravel, place a seat at one end, pile a few bricks on one side, and paint the wall behind with slogans. Before long that site could become as derelict as the one it replaced. Keith Cheng, who devised the Water Garden off

The Japanese Water Garden, in Covent Garden, specially designed by Keith Cheng to concentrate attention onto the water. An object lesson in how to design a tiny space into a much loved park. (Also cover photograph)

Shelton Street in Covent Garden, is emphatic that design of such spaces is most important. This Water Garden occupies about half an acre of formerly totally derelict land, overshadowed at one corner by the remainder of the enormous Odhams building. It is a considerable achievement to produce on that small site not only a garden which can accommodate the varied needs of kids playing football, people sunbathing, people watching the fountain, people walking around, or people having a meeting, but at the same time a garden which has an atmosphere and a life of its own. By the nature of its design, the fact that it is overshadowed by the Odhams monster goes virtually unnoticed, and the high buildings surrounding it on the other side make little impact. This has been achieved by deploying the architect's skill to focus the attention of anyone coming into the garden downhill onto the water and the bridge. This stretch of water is the key to the whole garden, because no matter where you are in that garden, you will be looking either across or downhill onto the water – the design and the landscaping compel one's eyes in that direction.

The success of the garden should be compared to that of other temporary gardens carried out by other community groups, which complain that the conflicting needs of old people wishing to sit out and kids playing football have led to clashes. There are no clashes in the Japanese Water Garden, and although the gates are always wide open so that anybody can walk, there is no vandalism. All in all, the Japanese Water Garden is an outstanding example of how to make a great deal out of a very little, and stands in amazing contrast to the expensively produced but boring 'public open spaces' with which we are so often provided by the authorities.

Note: This description may be taken as an obituary.

Improvisation

Another lesson to be learned from the Water Garden is improvisation. Most projects described in this book will have had help to some degree or other from industrialists who have provided materials, or help, free of charge, and providing the group knows precisely whch material it wishes, for what purpose and in what

A sad contrast to the Japanese Garden is the Tolmers Village community garden which, in this state, could almost be called blighted. Because something is carried out by voluntary effort should not mean that it requires any less attention than more official projects.

quantity, it is usually possible to obtain them. It is a matter of using ingenuity. For example, the Water Garden required mud to form the base of its water feature; where on earth could mud be obtained? Answer – London Transport Authority are excavating millions of tons of it a week in order to build the new Fleet underground line. Since London Transport have to dump this unwanted mud, they might be only too glad to deliver some of it to Covent Garden to help in what would be a socially worthwhile project. They were – they did – and one of the major obstacles was overcome.

This same resourceful attitude has led Martin Pawley to investigate the possibility of using rubbish and garbage for the construction of houses (see Chapter 6). In the same way, the Friends of the Earth put together and adapted two barrels on wheels which they had found lying on their derelict site in Waterloo for use as barrows and water collectors. A great deal of the 'making and doing' spirit was lost during the period of the affluent society in the 'sixties. We are forced to be more resourceful now.

Wall painting in London, brightening the neighbourhood of Gospel Oak.

References

1. Murals Kit (£1.00) by Michael Norton (Directory of Social Change, 14 Saltram Crescent, London W9).
2. *Soho Clarion* (the local community newspaper).
3. *Community Action* (16).
4. Victoria Square Competition, Birmingham Architectural Association, Birmingham Building Centre, Broad Street, Birmingham.
5. *Art into Landscape* catalogue, Arts Council.

Further useful sources

Your City has been Kidnapped, by Michael Norton, published by Community Service Volunteers, 237 Pentonville Road, London N1, price £1.00.
Community Festivals Handbook (John Hoyland), 20p from Young Volunteer Force Foundation, 7 Leonard Street, London EC2.
Pride of Place, Civic Trust, £2.00. An excellent handbook.

6 · BUILT PROJECTS

If all the steps suggested in this book have been followed so far, in a given neighbourhood, the result should, by now, be that it will have been cleaned up, there will be vegetables, flowers and creepers growing, and the morale of the local people will have been greatly restored. As an interim step, whilst waiting for the local authority to take further action, that is perfectly satisfactory. However, the local community may feel that it is worth undertaking further and more permanent action which could either supplement the local authority's actions, carry out necessary works which local authorities will not do, or perhaps even replace local authority action altogether.

Volunteer Organisations and Charities

A look at the vast range of work undertaken by charities throughout the country shows the extent to which the Government is incapable of undertaking all essential public functions. In the field of building and construction, two of the principal volunteer organisations – Shelter and the National Trust – undertake essential work in helping with housing advice and in caring for our historic heritage. Although these two organisations are the most famous in their fields, they are by no means the only ones, and those mentioned in this chapter are merely to be taken as representative of many.

A fairly recent newcomer to the task of preserving historic buildings is the Landmark Trust, founded to restore and repair ancient monuments. It raises the funds to do so by converting them into holiday homes and flats. By using this technique the Landmark Trust has managed to preserve from ruin or dereliction many splendid buildings, some of which had to be almost entirely rebuilt; and yet they have made no more than the normal call upon the Government using, for example, the Historic Buildings grants.

Historic Building Trusts

There are already a number of organisations which operate historic buildings trusts, and one such is the Suffolk Preservation Society. In 1973 it set up the Suffolk Building Preservation Trust, the purpose of which is to buy historic buildings, restore them and then sell them, hopefully at a modest profit, all of which has to be revolved so the more property can be purchased. According to its director, John Popham, the idea is excellent and works well when there is a property boom, but

'As we have found out in the last two or three years, such trusts are very slow moving when things are not so good. The other problem is that the Trust tends to get offered buildings which other people will not repair, either because of their position or because of their structural condition. This means working to a lower profit margin than an ordinary property developer might accept, and in some cases deciding not to make a profit at all. In operating the Trust, as a revolving fund for historic buildings, we are no different from other amenity societies up and down the country. However, we are in the process of widening our activities to include modern housing developments in infill situations. The Trust has been offered a 2-acre site in the village of Wetherden, and hopefully we will be shortly proceeding with the scheme. If this is successful we hope to be able to repeat this operation in the same way as for our historic buildings fund.'[1]

Up and down the country, old structures are being re-used as, for example, community centres, or local museums. A recent advertisement asked for volunteers to help in the restoration of Penrhos Court, near Kington in Herefordshire. The Court, consisting of a fine group of historic buildings with a hall to which later wings have been added, barns and other farm buildings, was taken over in 1972 by a group of enthusiasts who hope eventually to restore the entire complex. So far, an eighteenth-century stone barn has been converted into a restaurant, another two barns are being restored as office storage space, and a market garden has been created to provide flowers and vegetables. Similar work has been undertaken in Devon, where a mediaeval farmhouse complex is being restored, by child labour, to a youth and community centre. The children are volunteers from London who are paid 50p a day along with travel, accommodation and food, all under the supervision of an architect and a vicar. In addition to the advantages of being in a beautiful part of the country, the children learn how to mix cob, lay stones, rafters and carry out other essential building work. Not surprisingly, there is no shortage of volunteers.

Voluntary Labour

Just as there is no shortage of people to *organise* major developments, there is little shortage of people prepared to work on them. Volunteer labour has got well beyond the stage of putting a few bricks together or erecting the odd mud wall.

The Waterways Recovery Group is an offshoot of the Inland Waterways Association which has been responsible for a quite remarkable change in public attitude over the last twenty-four years towards the preservation, repair and eventual use of the British canal system. Since the Government seems to regard canals as a leisure activity and thus keeps the British Waterways Board (a government body dealing with canals) perpetually under-financed, volunteers must perform most of the major works and it was to co-ordinate and direct these works that the Waterways Recovery Group was set up. It has already a notable record for recovering and restoring various canals, and the recent restoration of the dangerously crumbling Stratford canal is a good case in point. The owners of the canal, the National Trust, did not have enough funds for essential and urgent works; consequently between October 1975 and March 1976 the WRG organised a blitz recovery. There was no lack of volunteers, and an average of 30, although sometimes reaching as high as 80, volunteers turned up every weekend. These volunteers came from almost every IWA branch, all WRG units, and a vast number of canal societies. The owners provided 1,500 steel sheet piles, the IWA granted £1,500 which assisted with the purchase of a punt, and volunteers carried out something like £15,000 of work for a total expenditure from all sources of £4,000 – a saving of almost 75 per cent.

Co-operative Warehouses and the problem of Small Industries

The rate of redevelopment in London and other major cities was, until recently, so great that the smaller users were being gradually forced out. The reason for this was as follows: until the Second World War, the pattern of development – certainly in London – was normally a matter of rehabilitating or redeveloping at the end of the lease cycle, usually a 99-year lease cycle. Thus it was that there were always buildings which were either newly built or newly rehabilitated (and therefore at the top of their market value) and always buildings at medium lease, and always buildings coming towards the end of their lease and thus in poor condition and at low rental. This pattern obviously depended on a stable rate of redevelopment – about 1 per cent per annum, so that an entire spectrum of leaseholds existed. Since the war, the redevelopment rate of Central London at any rate has been far higher than 1 per cent and in some areas reached 5 per cent per annum. This (in theory at any rate) could have had the result that in 20 years entire districts would either have been rebuilt or rehabilitated with the inevitable result that there would be less and less accommodation available at the lower end of the market. Government and local authorities never faced up to this problem, and certainly never came to the logical conclusion that redevelopment should either have been restricted to existing plot sizes only, or that only 1 per cent of the ground area should be developed each year. Thus it was that the entire central areas of large towns and cities became vulnerable to the large-scale user.

5 Dryden Street

Since the rents for accommodation in newly built office space were for too high for most small users – particularly professional offices – architects Rock Townsend converted a warehouse at 5 Dryden Street, Covent Garden for use as offices, on a co-operative basis, by smaller users such as architects, designers, quantity surveyors, engineers, model builders, landscape architects, and journalists. All of them had a say in the manage-

Volunteers from the Waterways Recovery Group using heavy equipment in their emergency restoration of the Lower Stratford Canal.

ment committee and they all paid for communal services (such as telephone, coffee machines, and committee rooms). This project has now been running successfully for almost four years, with some 30 firms operating within it. One of the original aims was the cross-fertilisation between firms and this has been achieved with considerable success. As a result, Rock Townsend have recently opened a successor in Chiswick. This time the Barley-Mow warehouse (the original Sanderson Wallpaper warehouse) has been converted into space for studios and workshops which should eventually provide room for some 250 people; but the aim is to broaden the base beyond professional firms, and over a third of the space is intended for craft or light industrial firms which are offered a preferential rent; £4.75 per square foot per annum as opposed to £8.75 for the design studios. In both of these cases the character of the building itself has created a pleasant atmosphere and contributed to the success of the venture.

WITH THE HOUSE AT THE OTHER END OF THE GARDEN, CHARLES'LL GET QUICKER TO THE STATION EVERY MORNING !

The advantages of self-building (see p. 91).

The Clerkenwell Workshops Project

Clerkenwell is a district once famous as the home of highly skilled watch and clock makers just north of the old City wall of London, which has been decaying since the war. The workshop project has converted an elderly school repository with some 35,000 square feet inside into work space at a low rent for light industrial users.

'The intention is to show that such projects can act as "pump primers" to blight areas, stimulating further initiative, conserving the existing urban character, creating local employment, encouraging apprenticeship, setting up an experimental nursery for further local projects and, above all, learning by doing.'[2]

The Clerkenwell Workshops already contain a gilder, watch and glass maker, glass beveller, diamond mounter, stained leaded glass maker, printer, silver toy/box maker, printer, 3 manufacturing jewellers, die sinker, watch-strap maker, silversmith/jeweller, theatre prop maker, luthier, 4 gold/silversmiths, fine metal caster, furrier, leather case maker, opthalmic instrument maker, manufacturing optician, engraver and a wood turner. Out of 29 firms listed, 23 represent local traditional skills, and 20 of these were existing local firms. The venture is self-financed, based upon renting out the workshops – at the moment costed at £2 per sq ft inclusive – and the day-to-day administration is undertaken by a resident management team. Communal facilities such as essential information exchange, exhibition area, marketing facilities, and magazine production are available, and there are close links with local residents.

One should compare these ventures with shared facilities and encouragement for cross-fertilisation, with the industrial estates which now litter the outskirts of towns and cities to which small firms such as the ones mentioned were often relegated once they were cleared out of their historic locations by planners. Although there are tremendous opportunities for industrial estates to provide shared facilities and shops, they are usually merely a cluster of unrelated businesses in a miserable traffic-dominated environment a long way from the most primitive facilities and isolated from normal life and shopping.

Mike Franks, one of the originators of the Clerkenwell project, maintains that

'The level of demand for reasonably priced commercial and industrial floor space in about 250–500 square foot units in the inner City is still very high, and the potential is still there (several million square feet around the Clerkenwell area alone) much of which must be capable of having a similar project approach to our own. We will be able to offer some workshops suitable for two people to work in for £10 per week, inclusive. Anyone who cannot work with those costs can hardly expect to operate a trading concern anywhere.'[2]

The Rotherhithe Project

Rotherhithe is an ancient seamen's town on the south bank of the Thames in East London which fell on evil days after being included in a Comprehensive Development Area soon after the last war. Many of its fine historic buildings and sea-captains' houses have already been demolished, and the retention of its remaining historic character – around the eighteenth-century church of St Mary's, the Mayflower pub, its few old houses and stone-flagged alleyways – depends to a large extent upon the re-use of a group of early nineteenth-century warehouses including the Hope Sufferance Wharf complex. This consists of two warehouses, a stable block and a granary, which have been taken over by the newly formed Industrial Buildings Trust. The Trust persuaded Southwark Council to buy a lease on the warehouses and then issue a compulsory purchase order on the freehold. The Council was also prepared to advance capital on the restoration (in return for two Council members being on the Trust itself) and further finance came from various charitable foundations, industry, and from public bodies.

The riverside warehouse has now been converted into a dance studio with other facilities for the Beshara Design Studio; and the Frobisher Institute of Adult Education proposes to use the rest of the stable block as a co-operative for craftsmen, also providing classes for local residents, with the possibility of apprenticeships. Another nearby warehouse, which was in use as a theatre, has been taken over and that part not used by the theatre is now

Rotherhithe, showing the warehouses which have been and which are soon to be converted into studios, theatres and the like. The Mayflower pub on the right is worth a visit.

The centrepiece of the Brunel project in Rotherhithe. Volunteers have cleared the area in front, and plans are in hand to convert this old pumping house into a museum of tunnelling.

rented out in small units at £3.50 per week, a rent which covers not only the ground rent but provides some working capital for improvements.

All these warehouse conversions have run into trouble with various regulations – particularly fire and health regulations and the cost of meeting these in the granary alone cost £129,000.[3] There will obviously have to be a reconsideration both of regulations and of their enforcement if these ventures are to become more widespread (this matter is dealt with more fully in Chapter 10).

Brunel Project

Also in Rotherhithe is to be found the four-year-old Brunel Exhibition Project whose aim is to restore the old engine and pumping house, first used for the excavation of Brunel's Thames Tunnel, into an exhibition displaying not only the history of the Tunnel but also tunnelling techniques. To accompany this, the Project has published an excellent booklet about the Tunnel and of Rotherhithe. Since the Project was the first attempt to redress the decline of Rotherhithe, it can probably be credited with creating the impetus which is now leading to all the other restoration projects in the area. The care, husbandry and protection of historic areas lie with the local Council – in theory, but in this instance, as in so many others, it is *voluntary* endeavour, albeit with Council support, which is turning the tide of dereliction.

Sanford Co-operative Project

In 1967, the London University Union published a report outlining the case for co-operative student residences, which argued that badly needed housing for students and others should be provided by a new housing scheme run according to Canadian examples. About a year later, the Student Co-operative Dwellings (SCD) was formed; after a further year, it was registered as a Housing Association and a charity; and three years later it was finally invited to submit a pilot scheme for co-operative student dwellings on a 1-acre site at Sanford Street, London SE14, which had been rejected by Lewisham Council as being unsuitable for family accommodation. After yet further delay, Sanford Co-operative dwellings were completed, and opened by Lord Goodman in 1974. The scheme provides 14 self-contained houses, each designed for ten single people, and six self-contained bedsitter flats for couples. Each house is fully equipped – 10 bedrooms each with its handbasin; 2 bathrooms, 3 WC's and a farmhouse kitchen.

Half of the cost of lease purchase and development was borrowed from Housing Corporation, and the other half from an insurance company, both loans repayable over 40 years, with the insurance company having first security on land and buildings. The variable rate of interest was reduced by the option mortgage tax relief from about 11 per cent to 7.4 per cent, and the resulting rent (October 1974) was £7 for a single person and £10 for a couple – probably marginally below the going rate at that time, and excellent value by now. A grant sufficient to cover the cost of the furnishings was negotiated with the ILEA, in return for the Co-op agreeing that at least 57 of its members would be ILEA students. Further details of this scheme are contained in 'Housing Co-operatives'.[4]

Other Student Housing

Two other recently formed organisations provide homes for students, the first of which, Blawhurst, had its origins when two students were unable to find a flat to rent and, instead, put down a deposit on a small dilapidated house which they rewired, replastered, plumbed and damp-proofed. This house was then let to other students, and within three years the capital cost had been recouped. During these three years, other houses were bought and treated in the same way, and in 1970 Blawhurst was formed with a loan of £2,000 from the Students Union at Hull University. The firm now owns 35 houses, providing homes for 140 students at a rent of £3.75 each, below the local market rate.

The University and Polytechnic of Leeds, together with the two student unions formed Unipol, which repairs derelict houses that are to be demolished in the future. The scheme was started on an interest-free loan of £4,000 from the University and Polytechnic, matched by £4,000 from the Council, and Unipol has now provided some 220 bedspaces. At £2.70 per person per week, a four-bedroomed house will have paid for itself in two years. A long-term intention is to use the recently established Unipol Housing Association, which has recently received planning permission for a complex of 629 study bedrooms and 76 two- and three-person flats. It is thought to be the largest development of this kind in the country.

Self-Building in South London

A direct way of supplementing the Council's house building programme is , of course, to build your own house. Self-building is very much part of the British tradition, but the lack of cheap land, the proliferation of regulations, and the cost of materials has inhibited self-building, making it more of an oddity than the norm. A recent report based on examples throughout Britain[6] describes how the problems of regulations, coupled with the desire to build something that would have a resale market value, and combined with frequently inefficient or off-putting site organisation have led self-builders to spend years of weekends and evenings building their dream houses and, because of this, sometimes ending up by loathing them.[5]

A major experiment in self-building is about to unleash itself in South London, one of whose purposes is to solve some of the problems just mentioned. The scheme involves Lewisham Council (which is providing the land), architect Walter Segal (who has designed the houses), the Council's Architects Department (who will be helping), and a number of energetic self-builders. The houses will be single-storey, flat-roofed houses, raised above the ground, and constructed with a timber frame which will be bolted together – a modern interpretation of ancient timber cottages. Segal considers the ability of the self-builder to begin immediately on his *own house* (rather than start by helping other people with *their* houses) is crucial to the success of the venture. 'The whole of self help hinges on organisation. Other (self build) schemes have taken a minimum of two or three years. I am

A Walter Segal designed house in Woodbridge, Suffolk, built by the occupants.

thinking in terms of weeks – eight weeks of working hours.' The design and materials have been carefully selected to aid the self-builders: the roof will be flat, since a pitched roof would cost more and increase the number of outside trades required; the self-builders will be expected to help each other in the erection and fixing of the main frames and supports; trades have been kept to a minimum – plumbers, drain layers, roofing contractors, joiners (to hang the doors) and possibly electricians. Any occupant skilled in these trades can, of course, do them himself – he is already expected to build the foundations himself.

Segal has had experience of people building their own houses to his designs and knows, for example, that an untrained husband and wife take about 1¼ hours to fit an 8-ft-long window. Considerable variety in each house will be possible so that the occupants will be able to stamp their personality upon it. This pilot scheme, is being watched with considerable interest by the Government, and at August 1976 prices, the total cost of each family (two-bedroomed) house will be about £4,000 – or a third of the normal cost of building.

The Council advertised the proposal in a newsletter to all residents, and arranged for a meeting to be held in July. Segal was expecting about nine or ten people and was pleased, if mildly horrified, to find some 90 people waiting to hear about the proposals, most of whom were young and full of enthusiasm. The major problem now will be one of how to select the lucky first few self-builders.

Self-Build School

One of the buildings in London which has already been designed and erected on Segal principles is at the Fleet School, Hampstead. The initiative came from architect Robert Howard, a tutor at the Bartlett School of Architecture who wished to involve his students in various direct building projects. Fleet School had allocated some space and about £3,000 for a parents' building, but could not afford it under normal methods at that time (1973).So, with three students (Jim Chapman, Frances Holles, Suzie Nelson) Howard designed a 1,000 sq ft wooden building (giving a price of £3 per sq ft, as against a normal contract price of the time, of £9 or £10 per sq ft). Plumbing and electricity cost another £500. The structure is a simple, flat-roofed timber building which stands on 3 ft by 2 ft concrete blobs. Great persuasion had to be used to convince the District Surveyor to permit these foundations rather than the more normal concrete raft or strip foundations, and the completed building has a strong visual affinity with those historic storage barns (which one can see in Sussex) which are perched on top of mushroom-headed stones. Howard and the students acted as the designers and directors, and the parents joined in as navvies. It took three summer months to complete, and the timber was cut to size and jointed on the site. The parents' room is on a three-year renewable licence, but it seems likely that it will become a permanent fixture. Howard considers that one interesting by-product is how fascinated the parents and non-architects became with how the thing was put together; somehow it made building much more understandable.

The Fleet extension almost completed.

Garbage Housing

Martin Pawley, author of the book *Garbage Housing*[6] which suggested that cheap materials for building houses could include throwaway items, recently began to build such a house in America. The Professor of Architectural History at Rennselear Polytechnic in Troy, put up $600 for a house, and the land overlooking the Hudson River, was presented by the Poly. A further $1,200 was spent on connecting the house to mains drainage. Pawley, with six students, took only six weeks to build the external shell and it consisted of the following: the frame of newsprint rolls obtained from the local newspaper which was discarding them at a rate of 150 per week; the walls of tin cans, discarded from the Poly's kitchen, along with 4,000 cans contributed by an American can company; the insulation of polyester waste from the local textile mill; and the roof structure of cardboard tubes which have been damp-proofed with waste plastic, covered with donated corrugated cardboard, which in turn will be covered with a layer of glass/fibre/sulphur. The house seems to conform to local regulations, and there are other clients in the offing.

Crumbles Play Castle

This next scheme, by contrast, is set in the grim environment to the north-east of the Kings Cross marshalling yards in London. It is a very poor area consisting mainly of derelict buildings, empty sites, a railway viaduct to the north, the canal to the south, and blocks of Council housing, old and new. By Bingfield Street, there used to exist a series of slab blocks of housing, built by the Victoria Dwellings Association to provide dwellings for the labouring classes. Officially called the Beaconsfield Buildings, they were known locally as Crumbles, and the last of them was finally demolished in 1971. Where they existed there now stands a castle.

Local residents had been looking for some time for a permanent site for an adventure playground, and one had existed on this site as a summer project. Coincidentally, three architectural students, Bob Hamment, Bob Parker and Cathy Davis, had designed a castle as a student project at the Central London Polytechnic, and the local people approached them wanting advice on a cheap building; a hall which could be used for events, lavatories, a kitchen, and a games room which the Committee could run. The kids wanted something different – a castle. The Central Poly recognised the development of the castle as a six weeks' project for the students (it lasted two years). Working weekends were advertised in *Time Out*, and the committee, and friends, and other locals helped with the levelling of the site and digging the foundations. The students produced detailed but simple work-sheets explaining what had to be done, and this stage was completed wholly by voluntary labour.

In the meantime, trouble was brewing with the planning authority. The local people wanted the castle where it now is, but the planners wanted any activity of that sort much further away from the housing, over by the main road (York Way). Conse-

Crumbles play castle, Islington.

quently the initial building work was begun without planning permission, and the planners only changed their mind (according to Cathy Davis) after a public meeting and a demonstration by the committee and the children. Other necessary permissions included Building and Fire Regulations. 'The District Surveyor needed to be convinced of every single stone, and Rod Mac-Donald (an engineer who gave help) had to design a structure with twice the strength really needed.'

As usual, many of the materials were donated by businesses: John Laing did the drainage, tower foundations, and laid the concrete slab; the GPO donated telegraph poles; Macready's gave steel; and local firms donated what they could. Some £4,000 was obtained from the Council's recreational budget 're-scheduled from trees', and by the time the castle was complete, the Council had in various ways contributed some £17,000. Most of the labour was provided free although in the later stages a wage of £2 per day was offered. The length of time of construction (over two years) meant that the initial enthusiasm of local parents to spend their evenings on the building site had died down, and that full-time, although lowly paid, builders were required. As usual improvisation was required and can be seen most ingeniously in the corbels which support the turret: these consist of concrete moulded in tyres.

Cathy Davis regards the local Council as a virtual opponent: 'It has taken us three years to build the castle, and the Council took three years to put up that corrugated sheeting around it. If we took down the sheeting and put up our own fence, the Council would demand the right to build their own fences, and would knock the other down.' Voluntary works, she considers, are largely things of the past, and in future adequate money will have to be found to pay for them. One source of money is the rescheduling of Council money which has been allocated to other activities (as is discussed in Chapter 9) particularly where more than one activity and their budgets can be combined. As Cathy Davis says, the local kids don't want to go to school, but they do like coming to the castle. Therefore, why should not some of the educational budget not help to pay for the castle, and have some teaching done there – where the kids do want to go?

In China, according to the exhibition which their Legation staged four years ago, schoolchildren help to build their own schools as part of the normal curriculum. There is no reason why this cannot be done in this country (particularly when one thinks of all those schools with grossly inadequate facilities, which have bought land for expansion which is still lying derelict through lack of cash). The Fleet School and Crumbles Play Castle are examples of structures which can be put up with unskilled labour as long as there is adequate professional expertise to hand. Even more compelling are the educational arguments. How much more effective an education in building and architecture (to say nothing of learning maths, precision, and a certain discipline) would it be if children had the opportunity to build buildings, than the talks which they are currently given on these subjects. That would be a *real* environmental education.

The Shorts Gardens Scheme

The Covent Garden Community Association persuaded the GLC to give a five-year lease on three buildings, in appalling condition in Shorts Gardens, for conversion into flats, and asked the Community Housing Association to organise the management and funding of the operation. As Jim Monahan (employed by the CGCA as one of the two architects designing the rehabilitation) put it 'the CHA had the knowhow to make it happen: and the CGCA knew their onions'. After ten months of protracted negotiations, the building work itself ('Cables were excellent') took four months, and the buildings, which were basically sound because they had had previously to cope with commercial uses, are now desirable properties. Many things about this scheme seem slightly too good to be true. Potential tenants were identified by the Community, and were able to specify particular items which they wanted in their flats such as hatches, and special tiles in the bathroom and so on, and would pay extra if necessary. The Housing Association left all the local problems to the Community – choosing the buildings, selecting the tenants, and providing the detailed specifications, in the way that should (but only rarely) happens. This scheme provides the only family housing in Covent Garden built since the last war where, like Soho, the officials believed that families would not wish to live. When the CGCA advertised the flats locally, there were over 75 applications for only five flats. The conversions have provided some very pleasant flats with a distinctive character, despite which the GLC still proposes (at the time of writing) that they shall be demolished in five years.

Originally, it was proposed that money would be available from the mini Housing Association Grants (HAG's) which are available for rehabiliating short-life property. Unfortunately, the maximum grant under this scheme would have been £7,200, whereas about £14,000 was needed (final cost £18,500) and so, the DoE finally agreed to support the scheme under the normal Housing Association grant (the difference between income and outgoings). The income from Shorts Gardens will total about £9,000 over five years, from very reasonable rents (averaging £7 per week), leaving a 50 per cent shortfall. The Housing Association and the CGCA next plan to have the Seven Dials area declared a Housing Action Area (on the grounds of the presence of a considerable quantity of empty residential property) for which the Government will give 90 per cent grants for conversion. If this is a success, Covent Garden would achieve an increase of 40 per cent in the availability of flats within five years.

The future of Covent Garden has been uncertain ever since it was decided to move the market to Nine Elms at Vauxhall, and a multi-disciplinary team was set up by the GLC over ten years ago to plan the future of the area. Ten years later, the local people are celebrating the conversion of some old houses into flats which they, themselves, have done; and one is almost tempted to agree with the CGCA's own sentiments:

'While the GLC has been planning, the Community has acted; we have built a community centre, started to build an indoor sports hall, taken over derelict land and made them into gardens, and initiated a street market in Drury Lane.

We want homes now, making the best of what we have, not grand plans that will never be realised. We do not need planners; we want builders, plumbers, and carpenters to get on with the job of getting Covent Garden back into a place where people can live and work.' (CGCA Press Release)

References

1. Letter from John Popham, Director, Suffolk Preservation Society to Charles McKean, 17 August 1976.
2. *Architectural Association Quarterly* (AAQ), Vol. 7, no. 4.
3. *Building Design.*
4. *Housing Co-operatives* (John Hands, published by SCD, price £1.50).
5. Alternatives in Housing? A report on self-build in Britain by students of the Architectural Association, sold by the AA Bookshop, 34–36 Bedford Square, London WC1
6. *Garbage Housing*, by Martin Pawley (Architectural Press).

7 · ORGANISATION

Many Councils regard local groups as troublemakers, and so if these groups are to be in a position to negotiate on more equal terms than at present with the authorities, then they require some permanent stake in their area. This chapter is therefore less concerned with structures which have or will be built, than with the organisation behind them, for it is the effectiveness of the organisation which will govern whether the spirit of self-help will endure beyond the completion of this building or that play-ground.

The Soho Society

The rise of the Soho Society to its present position as the local community organisation for trades, shops and residents of Soho is a very good example of what can be achieved. Until five years ago, the life of Soho had been draining away under the combined attack of office development, official neglect of its residential environment by the Council, and the general attitude that Soho was the sin centre of London. Indeed at the inaugural meeting of the Society, many of those present felt that it was too late to reverse this trend. The morale of the Soho Community was very low: rubbish was collected at 2 a.m., waking up local residents; most of the local facilities such as schools and laundrettes had closed; clubs and strip joints were creating a great deal of noise and unpleasantness throughout the night; there were several major areas of Soho coming up for development; and the Council itself had demolished streets for no specific purpose. The general attitude was that no *nice* person would really like to live in Soho, and that sooner or later all the residential accommodation would

be redeveloped, with alternative dwellings being provided elsewhere for those who were displaced. The first stage in the restoration of morale was the winning of some redevelopment
battles – particularly that over the John Snow site in Lexington
Street, and the saving of a row of early eighteenth-century
houses in Broadwick Street. The Society was also able to keep far
closer tabs on the development of the area, in such matters as
illegal changes of use from flats to offices, or the moonlight flit of a
strip joint from one basement to another, than the Council. Soon
clubs and strip joints were surprised to find that they were
reported for noise at night. In fact, the Soho Society was founded
just in time to revive the normal but decayed community
mechanisms, and has established a newspaper *Soho Clarion*, a
dancing team and a football club. But there are still threats: the
Council is keen to demolish the ancient blocks of Victorian flats,
although they are not prepared to provide new housing in Soho
themselves.

Like many local societies, the Soho Society is not without its
extroverts, and the day after Lord Goodman made his famous
speech calling for angry young men with fire in their bellies who
would help the aforesaid Lord Goodman solve the housing crisis,
Stephen Fry rang him to suggest that he should provide money
for a Soho housing association. He got it. Coincidentally seven
other people within the society had set up a co-ownership housing association (for which funds were unfortunately not available
– and the City Council was obstructive about providing land).
The two propositions merged into the Soho Housing Association
which is now registered with the Housing Corporation. Dickon
and Charlotte Robinson, who were among the originators of the
Housing Association, point out that the value of their own local
association is the power that it gives to local groups to provide
housing for local people. The prospect of a large, distant, housing
association taking over local endeavour is almost as inimical to
them as letting the Council take it on themselves, since the small
scale sensitive 'feel' of the operation is lost. The obstruction
encountered from the Council was based on the attitude that
Soho Housing Association was a 'bunch of amateurs'; the
'amateurs' won, and, the first scheme consisting of 27 flats in

Great Pulteney Street and Bridle Lane, has been granted planning permission; whilst another development of 30 more flats in Marshall Street has been submitted. Further schemes are being prepared for Royalty Mansions (Meard Street) and the St James's residences. If these schemes are successful, before very long the Soho Society will be the main housing authority in the Soho area. Another conservation society – the Camberwell Society has just taken steps in the same direction, by reviving a local, dormant housing association to promote house building and conversions in that district.

Co-operatives

A different form of initiative can be seen in co-operatives, which can be of several types: (*a*) a tenant co-operative managing a Council estate; (*b*) a co-operative managing the rehabilitation of a housing action area, most of the houses of which have been purchased by local authority (as in the Birnam Road area of Islington; (*c*) a co-operative which owns the building and the land itself, borrowing the money against the mortgage; and (*d*) a co-operative which sets up as a joint non-profit-making venture in business. An interesting tenant management co-operative is that recently set up by the Greater London Council in the St Katherine Estate, Wapping, East London. The Housing Rents and Subsidies Act 'enables a local authority to reach an agreement with a co-operative for the exercise by the latter at a particular estate of virtually all the local authority's housing powers without forfeiting government subsidy'. In the case in question, some 167 pre-1945 dwellings are involved, on an estate which was mostly empty awaiting modernisation which had to be dropped as a result of cuts. The Stephen and Matilda Tenants Association negotiated the establishment of this co-operative with the GLC, and will become responsible for the management and maintenance of the estate. The remaining tenants were given the choice to stay in the buildings and help with the co-operative or leave, and those tenants who had already left were given the choice to return. The co-operative will operate general management, the lettings, the collection of rent and rates, caretaking and day-to-day maintenance, whilst the landlord – the GLC – will remain owner, and contractor for specified works. The GLC will pay, to the co-operative, monthly 'an amount which in total will be equivalent to the pooled cost of management and maintenance per dwelling for an estate of that type' and it will be this money that the co-op will use to their own ends. A similar co-operative venture is proposed for the Juniper House, Kender Estate, Deptford, and for other estates. The Government's attitude towards co-operatives such as this is as follows:

'Co-operatives should not be seen simply as a means of relinquishing responsibility for problem estates or for functions which are proving troublesome.'

Purists may argue that the management co-op achieves little. They would be wrong. Tenants living in squalor have a chance to reverse these conditions as well as having the opportunity to decide things for themselves. How different this is from, say, the Council's attitude to tenants on the North Peckham Estate, London, where (*Building Design* reports) tenants are being *allowed* to choose the colour of their own front doors (*Building Design*, 19.11.76).

Fairhazel is a co-operative which owns a group of mansion blocks and houses in North West London, dating from about 1890, which they have bought with a mortgage from Camden Council. The mortgage also provides funds to do the repairs and rehabilitation which have become necessary through lack of maintenance, and Fairhazel is expected to bring the buildings up to a standard which will be sound for at least another 30 years. Of course, as everybody now realises, buildings such as these have an indefinite life as long as they are well maintained and meet the needs of the inhabitants. Being a co-operative, the inhabitants have a greater say in what it to be done than is normal, and the architects for the scheme have to have an office on site to advise, particularly in the evenings when tenants arrive home from work. It must be novel for the architects to have over 117 clients in a single development.

The finances are tortuous. The Government provided £605,000 to Camden Council which was lent to Fairhazel against a mortgage to purchase the freeholds. It might be questioned whether the capital purchase price was not too high for blocks of decaying mansion flats, or indeed whether the conversion cost which has been estimated at about £10,000 per flat is not excessive. These costs can be afforded since the Government is underwriting the difference between the rent income (or mortgage repayment) and the cost of the mortgage – which would come to almost 80 per cent of the total cost. Thus this scheme has a similar subsidy arrangement to that of Council housing, and can in no way be thought of as paying for itself. A more interesting exercise might have been to have tailored the amount of conversion exactly to what could be afforded: in other words *minimum change commensurate with reasonable living conditions*. Further and more elaborate changes could have been made when the individual tenant's income permitted, or when the co-operative collectively had managed to find some finance. There are still three advantages to this co-operative over the normal procedures of demolition and redevelopment: firstly, the great length of development time during which the land and buildings are empty is avoided and this accommodation will always be in use; secondly, the very fact of being members of a co-operative is stimulating participation and community spirit by the tenants – a feature not frequently remarked in new Council schemes; and lastly, even at a cost of £15,000 per flat, the scheme is probably cheaper than the Council cost of a new redevelopment.

The Black Road Scheme, Macclesfield

A completely different type of action was taken by local residents in the Black Road area of Macclesfield whose houses, dating mostly from 1813 to 1817, had been zoned for clearance in 1968 but which, as the result of lack of finance to implement the demolition, were still standing in 1972. By the time the clearance programme was resumed, a local residents committee had been set up with its own architect resident Rod Hackney, and a builder, Tom Lawton, who surveyed the 32 properties and put up the case that a General Improvement Area should be declared (under the terms of the 1969 Housing Act) rather than demoli-

The backs of the Black Road houses (before).

tion. They lobbied the local Council, and the Department of the Environment left the decision up to the local Council on the grounds that although the Department had doubts that the buildings were worth it, local conditions should prevail. Rod Hackney makes the significant comment

'The residents all along avoided any personal criticism of local government officers and elected representatives . . . their insistence on avoiding criticising individuals within the local authority had a great bearing on the outcome of the first fight to save their homes, and subsequently the successful management of the general improvement area.' (Royal Society of Health Conference on Housing Improvements.)

Finally, the Council approved a General Improvement Area on the grounds that the residents thought their homes were still viable, and were prepared to invest in them; and that the new legislation (namely the Housing Act 1969) had altered the situation on which the 1968 clearance order had been made. Council voted £250 per house for environmental works, provided tem-

The back area of Black Road (after), taken from slightly further back.

porary rented accommodation for those people whose houses were being improved, and were prepared to award maximum improvement grants where appropriate.

'The Black Road Area Residents Asociation planned the building operations so that many of their own residents participated in the actual construction tasks. They supervised the works during progress. They co-ordinated all activities relating to the work on site. They arranged financial help for the scheme and established tomporary housing for themselves whilst individual house improvement work commenced. Transport and removal facilities were arranged to and from temporary housing. . . . As there were no roads within the scheme the residents built a temporary road for the contractors so that they could gain access to the site, and for storing materials. This, of course, saved a considerable amount of money. Before the road could be built, all the residents had to dedicate over to the group part of their private land thus allowing the roadworks a route through what were previously their gardens. (This route has now been converted into an open area with paving, playspaces, seating, trees, flowers and shrubs). The sharing of land had other advantages. It allowed extensions to be built on former neighbouring land where difficulties arose in the planning of extensions. It did away with the old "rights of way" and especially the "rights of light".

The Local Authority needed convincing quickly that the Group had indeed put their money where their mouths were, and the residents needed something to show in a short space of time what they could achieve in actual construction terms. So, whilst the overall scheme was being planned, Rod Hackney converted his own house at 222 Black Road as a show house. The bricklayer in the group, Tom Lawton, took upon himself the role of main contractor, one of the electricians did the rewiring, other residents helped in the demolition of chimney breasts, knocking down walls, carting away rubbish . . . and they also helped in redecoration works. After three months, the show house was complete. The Council were impressed with the first conversion.

Building prices had soared since the scheme was first thought of, and to keep pace with these inflationary trends and not to overspend on the amount of mortgages being offered, the residents have had occasionally to do more of the house improvement work themselves. For example, if the house costs increase by £50, then the resident for the house concerned offers his labour to ths contractor for a couple of days resulting in the appropriate saving . . . most of the residents worked on the building site in the evenings and weekends.

No single house is the same as any other. The completed improved houses all reflect the wishes and requirements of the residents. . . . The windows and doors are all different; there are many types of staircase . . . the kitchen layouts are all different . . . some residents had shower cubicles, others a bath . . . many wanted fireplace features.

The Local Authority, on their part, have acted responsibly in their interpretation of the building regulations for older buildings. Rigid, inflexible standards have not been asked for. . . . The results have satisfied everybody. This was not a simple task of upgrading older houses to the 12 point standard as laid down in the 1969 Housing Act, but rather a detailed exercise in accommodating the wishes of the individual residents, and at the same time producing new homes for them to live in and of which they could be proud, and call the result their own.' (Black Road Area Residents Association, writing in *Community Action* magazine, June–July 1974.)

This scheme was subsequently given an award for good design in housing (GIA Category) by the Department of the Environment. These buildings are not large, not spacious, and are very close together; yet the combined efforts of the tenants, coupled with the fact that they did not wish to leave their houses, however cramped, have produced an environment of which the tenants and occupants are themselves responsible, and that is the ultimate aim. Rod Hackney's conclusions from this scheme are as follows:

(a) The rectangular site chosen for the pilot scheme proved ideal in its internal arrangement of spaces for a successful environmental improvement scheme. It showed that without any works to the surrounding roadways a successful environmental scheme could concentrate on simply tidying up the 'backs', the areas between terraces and making the house improvement and environmental improvements compatible with each other.

(b) By concentrating on a small compact area and making sure that all the houses were improved the Group were able to ensure that their houses, being within self-contained boundaries, would not prejudice future plans for immediately surrounding areas.

(c) The Group decided at the outset to establish a successful precedent. Once this had been achieved they then expected the future to take a similar course as long as the financial incentives were still available for house and area improvement.

(d) Rather than sit back on their laurels once they had saved their homes, they simply transferred the energy displayed in their campaign to the practical implementation of the house and area improvement scheme.

(e) Lastly, they embarked on a campaign to save their homes knowing that they were right in what they wanted. They were willing to sacrifice personal gain to see the joint effort succeed. In many respects they took most of the people they dealt with by surprise. The Group's single minded aim to get on with the job of improving their homes and the energy they displayed in achieving this aim, guided by their basic common-sense attitude, were the hallmarks of their achievements. (*Taken from the transactions of the Royal Society of Health's Conference on Housing Improvements.*)

Although there have been no further schemes similar to Black Road as yet, it is possible that the approach will grow in popularity and there are indications that Prospect Road GIA in Cambridge, the Heckford Park GIA in Poole, Dorset, and a few others may develop along similar lines. In London there have been a number of public enquiries into slum clearance (part 3 of the Housing Act 1957) which have subsequently been won by the residents who then organised a co-operative rehabilitation of their houses. Chris Whittaker is a professional involved with such cases, one of which was an enquiry into a group of houses – including 18 owner-occupied houses – close to central London. The inspector confirmed the compulsory purchase order (against the wishes of the residents) but the Secretary of State dissented on the grounds that the houses were 'improvable for a number of years'. Whittaker is now involved in helping the residents to establish a co-operative housing association, through which improvements to the houses will be effected. It may well be that this approach will put a far smaller charge on public funds than if a redevelopment scheme had been implemented. Details of recent developments contained in the postscript.

Covent Garden Community

Occasionally some of the objectives of the Council might be supported by the local community whilst there will still be disagreement as to how these objectives should be implemented. The Covent Garden Community Association (with the help of a grant from the Monument Trust towards the cost of employing professionals), has carried out a survey of nine sites which the GLC's Covent Garden team are considering for possible redevelopment in the future. The aim of the GLC to increase the amount of housing in the area is strongly supported by the community association; the difference lies in how this increase is to be achieved. The Community Association reports that the GLC's initial studies make a presumption of demolition and development whereas their own alternative schemes show that the housing gain can be achieved without any disruption for existing businesses or residents. Furthermore, although the GLC envisages a possibility of demolishing listed buildings, the Community Association programme would involve the rehabilitation of these listed buildings and the use of empty sites. Although admittedly partial, the Covent Garden Community Association's press release is worth quoting as a statement of aims:

'The Covent Garden Community Association has produced alternative plans for every one of the GLC's redevelopment sites. The approach in all these alternative schemes has been to retain the existing businesses and residents, yet still provide substantial housing gains through re-habilitation, developing vacant sites and converting empty properties. This approach is cheaper, less destructive and more in keeping with the needs and the desires of the locality.'

The Community were lucky that they managed to raise funds to pay for professional advice, so that genuine alternatives could be considered. *Late news:* it is nice to report that the GLC committee has now endorsed the proposals suggested by the Community Association.

Advice in Glasgow

There is a major psychological difference between a group iden-tifying its own problems and trying to solve them (as in Maccles-field or Covent Garden) and a body of outsiders coming in to give advice. The latter is particularly necessary where local people are so bludgeoned by Councils that they do not believe that there is any alternative open to them but to accept Council proposals. In Glasgow for instance, the official attitude towards tenement buildings has been that they constitute an out-of-date form of housing and should be demolished – no matter what the tenants or owners might think. A recent song puts this well:

> 'They're pullin' doon the tenement next tae oors,
> Tae send us oot tae Green Belt, trees an' floors;
> But we dinnae want tae go,
> And we've surely telt them so,
> Oh they're pullin' down the tenement next tae oors . . .

ASSIST is a research unit of Strathclyde University which was founded in 1972 following a thesis by Raymond Young (in 1969) on voluntary tenement improvement, and the practical ex-perience he had gained from moving to Govan in 1970. Govan was one of Glasgow's notorious Comprehensive Development Areas, and one of the centres of the near-defunct ship-building industry. Glasgow Corporation was eventually persuaded to declare part of it a Treatment Area, and no less than its Lord

Provost opened the Assist shop. A study of 200 houses revealed that a high percentage of owners and tenants wished to remain in the area despite the grim environment caused by twenty-five years' decay and neglect. The architecture shop soon found that local residents did not distinguish between the types of advice required, and the 'shop' had to have other professionals available to give advice on matters ranging from rent rebates, where to find a plumber, to the break-up of marriages. Soon it developed in to a mini local authority (in the best sense of this term) in that on certain days of the week officials from the corporation visit the shop where they can meet enquirers and give help. Thus, apart from the valuable work in pioneering tenement rehabilitation and public participation, ASSIST has pioneered a method by which the skills of the Council can be made available at a very local level, avoiding all the inhibiting factors usually associated with 'going up to the Council'. Significantly, in Glasgow of all places, the tenant or occupier is now choosing himself whether to stay in a tenement and have it improved, or to move to accommodation elsewhere. The concept of tenant freedom of choice is a bitter pill for a dictatorial corporation to swallow, and it is to be hoped that it has not merely lodged, for the time being, in the corporation's throat.

8 · ACTION GROUPS, COMMUNITIES AND CO-OPERATION

The terms Action Group, Local Community Group, Community and Amenity Society have been used throughout this book, and it is necessary to investigate precisely what they mean if powers of supplementing or replacing Council work are to be devolved.

Most action or community groups have been formed in response to some direct threat, usually that of redevelopment, and as long as the threat persists participation tends to remain high. Problems arise when such groups try to translate local enthusiasm for *preventing* something happening, into *proposing* something new or into taking on some permanent duties. As a rule, action groups are not organised for continuing administration.

Different again are the civic and amenity societies (the title seems to be interchangeable) which are generally conservationist in attitude, although some share the beleaguered attitude of the action groups (the only difference between them being the quality of the respective areas the groups were formed to protect). However, many of the thousand-odd such societies registered with the Civic Trust *do* have the facility for on-going administration and, as has been seen in Chapter 6, some have set up building trusts and similar ventures. Tenants associations, ratepayers associations, Chambers of Commerce and the like organisations are what their titles imply, and usually display the narrowness of interest one might expect. There can be some surprising exceptions.

The proliferation of such groups makes local Councils chary of public participation, since they claim that it is not possible to

know which really speaks for the community. For example there
are two local bodies, both of which claim to speak for the local
community in Covent Garden – the officially supported, widely
based Forum on the one hand, and the active, successful and
pushing Covent Garden Community Association on the other.
Predictably they do not always see eye to eye. Councillors maintain that such groups only represent the active vociferous minor-
ity, leaving the silent majority completely indifferent; perhaps
they should look to their *own* elections in this case, where, very
frequently, voting figures are unlikely to represent the majority
of the total electorate, and in London only 29 per cent of the
electorate! In reality, councillors are concerned at the erosion of
their power and prestige, and are therefore hardly likely to welcome any change. In view of which it is not surprising that
Edinburgh District Council, for example, recently voted against
the establishment of community councils.

The reason why local participation is restricted to a handful is
firstly that the power of doing anything has been removed from
local levels to distant Castles of Despair which are impossible to
influence and dangerous to lobby unless you want to join the
black-list; secondly this remoteness of power has led to a gap
between the act (voting for a councillor) and the physical result (a
new housing development in 15 years). This gap between power
and its consequence will have to be closed if people are going to
participate; conversely, if local people were aware that a parish
council or other local organisation were going to take over lettings
for a local housing estate (as is the case in Russia) they would
participate soon enough. The experience of co-operatives, discussed in previous chapters, indicates that where power is manifest the participation rate may rise to 75 or 80 per cent. It is human
nature that it is unlikely to go higher.

Common Interest

Many actions groups and pressure groups believe that they have
totally different aims to other action groups, and some take on an
overtly political stance. For example, the magazine *Community
Action* (a valuable source of help and information) appears to take

Possible treatment for the Rochdale canal.

a Marxist approach whilst *Undercurrents* is anarchist, and the Civic Trust newsletter is regarded by some – particularly on the left – as conservative (just as conservation societies are generally considered to be the preserves of wealthy retired colonels. To test this view, I asked Arthur Percival in how many of the thousand Civic Trust registered societies were retired colonels active; and the answer (after a long pause) 'Possibly two.').

A great deal of common interest is obfuscated by political irrelevance, and this common interest is that the members of all societies are volunteers, and that they are passionately interested in improving local conditions. A recent editorial in *Community Action* (no. 13) said 'If Community action is to have any meaning at all then it must be based on people sharing their experiences with others who are fighting the same issues.' The magazine was referring to specific issues such as housing conditions and slum clearance programmes, but *effectively the fundamental issue, which those groups are fighting is the same one as all groups are fighting – namely the problem of remoteness and the lack of power to influence the local environment* (environment in its widest sense). Some groups are extremely unwilling to share their experiences for the benefit of others, and in certain cases this verges on paranoia. In 1975, the RIBA 'London Exhibition' which was being held in the Covent Garden Flower Market, invited the local community association to explain how the association had achieved its aims, converted its warehouse, dug its garden, planted its trees. The association refused to participate. Many of those interviewed in the process of compiling this book were emphatic that they and *only they* could have done what they did, and that what was the use, therefore, of telling other people about it? A notable exception to this were the Friends of the Earth who appeared willing both to inform and learn from others.

It is a sad fact that action groups tend to attract into them a certain type of person who is *competitive* in nature, frequently with the attitude 'My community is better than yours', or 'Our festival is more successful than yours'; and needless competition between local groups and personalities leads to yet more squandering of that valuable asset – volunteer enthusiasm – and yet greater weakness in the face of those distant remote Councils. If community and action groups could only concentrate on what they had in common rather than upon the organisational or ideological differences, very much more would be achieved.

Local Organisations

There is an essential functional difference between an action group and a permanent organisation, and this might be best explained by an analogy taken from recent events at the Ffestinniog Railway, which is a voluntary effort to rebuild a railway line through the hard hills of North Wales. Until recently the work was carried on entirely by volunteers who spent weekends in a labour camp – the equivalent of an action group. Now that a successful conclusion can be perceived in the distance, the

Traffic management: Royds Street scheme, Rochdale Industrial General Improvement Area.

authorities are prepared to back the scheme and have provided money for full-time staff; instead of the staff helping volunteers, volunteers now help full-time staff. Many volunteers have been put off by this change, and have retired from the project. In other words, the Ffestinniog project has now a permanent life of its own. It has ceased to be an action group and has become an organisation. There is a similarity between this development and the relationship between the Waterways Recovery Group (volunteers) and the British Waterways Board (officials). Action groups certainly require money and help, but for certain types of activities – only rarely do they require permanent staff.

A distinction should also be made between the widespread local organisations – such as parish and community councils – and groups with limited aims such as tenants associations, co-operative management committees, and all groups which see themselves as pressure groups.

Parish and Community Councils

The smallest *official* unit of Government is the parish council of which there are some 8,000 in England and Wales, ranging in numbers of electors from 98 to 42,000. These councils were given increased statutory powers after the recent local Government reorganisation – which was just as well since the reorganisation made local Government a complete misnomer. The local Council is now either geographically distant or psychologically light years away from local problems. Parish councils are directly elected organisations, and it was proposed that they should have city cousins called 'neighbourhood' or 'community' councils. It is interesting to note that it would be possible to have over ten parish/community councils of the large 30,000 electorate within the territory of *one* so-called 'local' London Borough Council. It seems that many parish councils are not aware of their duties or of their rights, and that their effectiveness varies. However, where parish councils have taken a grip upon their duties, the results can be excellent.

'Their authority is not to be measured solely by the extent of their legal functions or the size of their funds – which are sometimes large. They are an organ of local opinion – – – they are the only local councils in close and regular touch with their electorates – – – they have always had special concerns of a peculiarly local character.'[1]

Apart from their duties, parish councils have widespread powers. They can impose a rate on their own parish council area, which is levied by the district Council as part of the general rate but repaid back to the parish council for its own use. Parish councils are also at liberty to borrow money, and are sufficiently responsible bodies to assume other duties such as taking over the lease of premises above shops (see Chapter 10). Locally organised projects and activities may also be better and more sensitively managed than those promoted by some distant Council although some of the better exceptions to this rule are discussed later.

'The idea that "Government" can do everything that "Government" can solve all the problems, that "Government" can look after the people is a poverty stricken idea; the effectiveness of Government is precisely determined by the degree to which it helps or hinders people to look after themselves.'[2]

Local conditions will undoubtedly determine which type of organisation is chosen, but since the greater the change proposed the less is likely to happen, the following pattern is suggested as one which could be integrated with remarkably little effort into the existing system. Therefore the parish (or community) council should be given wide powers of determining the future of a local area and at the same time gather under its general administration all the specialist sub-groups, action groups, pressure groups and the like. Details of how this might work are given in Chapter 10. There is not much risk that parish councils will adopt the less likeable features of district or borough Councils, since the parish boundaries are tight, the number of electors is restricted, and as long as the parish council does not take on too many permanent employees it will always remain something of a voluntary body.

E. F. Schumacher (author of *Small is Beautiful*) recently wrote:

'The *spending* of money is something which requires the "human" touch, the very thing that bureaucracy cannot have no matter how diligent and compassionate the bureaucrats, as individuals, are wishing to be. It follows that one of society's foremost tasks is to devise a system by which (to put it crudely) government collects the necessary funds for non-governmental, voluntary organisations to spend them.' (*People's Power*)

If control of expenditure on a local scale becomes a local matter, the district or county Councils will be changing their function from the *doers*, to those who enable other people to do things. The absence of any significant full-time employees (save in an advisory capacity from the district Council) will help parish councils to keep their spontaneity and close contact with local people. It is for this reason that one suspects the genuine value of Home Office projects such as the Community Development Project which provides finance for full-time employees, grandly titled 'Research Fellows' and others going to work in a local district. There is more than just a hint of well-paid people coming in from the outside to tell the local people what they need.

The Reintegration of the Community

Action groups are not the only organisations which have an interest in a locality, and it is time that all parts of the community – the Council, the local organisations, parish councils, industry and commerce – became reintegrated. Many local projects have been helped considerably by the donation of materials or time or work by large companies, and it is normal to consider such donations as charitable with no further of longer term significance. Not so. Companies and businesses operating in a given area and drawing the work force from that area will have their output affected if the environment of the area remains unpleasant. Thus there are both social and economic arguments for industry and commerce helping to maintain a decent environment. When Crittals were building their factory village for their employees they stated:

'What an anti-social spirit it is that urges that the mental and physical well being is of no concern of the firm. Indeed it is, or should be, the first and foremost consideration of every commercial and industrial enterprise.'[3]

It is the same spirit that prompted the largest employer in Street, Somerset, Clarks Shoes, to provide (free of charge) the land which was required for a by-pass for Street. How lucky Street is as, say, compared to Saxmundham (Suffolk) which has been refused a by-pass (sorely needed) on the grounds that the town, like Street, is not large enough. Most towns have a prominent builder or a prominent business which has a vested interest in the well-being of that town that could be approached in a co-operative spirit to see what could be achieved jointly. Examples are Bulmers, associated with Hereford, Boots with Nottingham, Rowntrees with York, or Keiller with Dundee. Only recently Keith Showering (of Babycham fame) provided Shepton Mallet with a new town centre.

In the past, where a site has become available for redevelopment, it has been presumed that the varying demands on that land are conflicting, and that the purchaser with the greatest power will purchase. What is rarely considered is whether all the conflicting businesses in fact have interests in common, and that a co-operative venture could achieve the required aims. For example, there is a site of five acres in the centre of Bury St Edmunds which has recently become vacant. The site is likely to be purchased by the district Council, which feels that it has not got very much money to spare; there are no really active local developers, and in the normal event, this site could become blighted. However, taking the co-operative approach, a working group could be set up consisting of the Council, the local people and conservation societies, the local industry and businesses, the local shops, and the local tourist and hotel trade. It could well be that if a combined mixed development were promoted which could provide something for some or all of these varying groups, the result would achieve a cross subsidy which could subsidise lower rented accommodation at the one end, as against the higher rate producing shops and hotel or tourist provisions on the other.

In Poole, Dorset, the largest industrial employer, Hamworthy Engineering, has recently joined forces with the Council and the housing association to provide 103 new houses for skilled workers and public service employees on a 10-acre site in the town. Schumacher's pamphlet, already quoted above, gives a more startling example:

'Until last year, the downtown district and the tax base of Lima, Ohio, were disappearing at approximately the same rate. The bus system had broken down, the turreted old railway station had to close, and the streets were full of pot holes. Then a man got himself elected as mayor with the slogan "Let's get together and make Lima better – better without any new taxes." In a surprisingly short time he did just that: he started a new money making transit system with hired buses . . . he has arranged for welfare recipients to clean the streets and plant shrubs, ivy and trees. He has encouraged the neighbourhood youth corps to patch up the old train station thereby enabling (the railway line) to reopen it for passenger traffic. . . . Essentially, the mayor's strategy is to *merge public funds with private effort. . . .*' (my italics)

The Norwich Example

A slightly less esoteric but equally successful scheme was launched by Norwich City Council in 1974, the aim of which was to stop the decline of that section of the mediaeval city which lay across the River Wensum. The scheme involved local people, conservation groups, church congregations, schools, developers and youth groups; the latter cleaned eyesores, the Council rehabilitated its own properties and constructed new housing, and in summary the success of this scheme, which won a European Architectural Heritage Year Award 1975, was based on the co-operation between interested parties in a common aim.

The Rochdale Example

All right for famous historic towns you might say, but what about the ordinary drab environment in which most of us have to eke out our existence? It is beginning to look as though the Metropolitan Borough of Rochdale has the answer to that (although the example of Black Road, Macclesfield, already discussed, should not be forgotten). Like many Northern towns, Rochdale has several old and run-down industrial areas:

'There are many industrial sites with a general inheritance of non-planned growth that have no regard for the disastrous environmental

Wellfield Mill, Rochdale, which has now been reinstated. The outbuildings will be demolished and replaced with landscaped areas.

effect on adjoining residential areas, or the depressing psychological effect on employers and employees who are obliged to spend the major part of their lives in these areas.'[4]

The solution chosen was that the Council declared the first ever industrial improvement area in order to test whether the available grants would cover the necessary work. It is a reflection on the size of Council territories, however, that the area of Rochdale which has been selected is but a small part of Rochdale territory as a whole, and the specific study area within the GIA is smaller yet. The Council's approach seems to be humble, pragmatic and very wise. The initial report on the scheme recognises the need for a sense of pride, for some quick results before enthusiasm evaporates and, far from choosing an easy area, they selected a district which has 'just about every kind of land use – major engineering factories, mills, scrap yards, a dairy, a bakery, motor repairers

Rochdale. A typical scene further along the street, showing parking problems.

and an abattoir'. The key statement in the Council report is 'The success of this scheme will depend largely upon the good will and enthusiasm of the industrialists within the area,' and the Council have suggested that the industrialists be represented on the steering committee.

The Borough has also involved the Canal Society in a scheme which, with the help of the job creation programme, will result in the restoration of six miles of canal. By setting up a local steering committee, with professional advice from the Council, Rochdale is virtually setting up a community council (albeit non-elected) and where the project is larger than can be coped with entirely by a parish council, the Rochdale approach of co-operation is very much to be welcomed.

Conclusion

Action, Community, Conservation and Pressure groups are likely to remain so, and fulfil a valuable function. However, on-going supervision of a local area is best undertaken by a parish council in consultation with them and the district Councils should be prepared to devolve to parish councils power and money for parish councils to look after themselves. It is ironic that parish councils have power, but generally speaking, exist only in rural or small town areas. There is a far greater and more urgent need for their city cousins, the community councils, few of which (as far as I know) yet exist. These should have similar powers to parish councils, such as that of raising rates, and it is a great pity that their establishment depends upon the voting of the councillors of existing districts (who have an innate bias against supporting such organisations). Finally, the policy of co-operation between all sectors of the community should be fostered and encouraged since it will provide resources where none at present exist, and will restore self-respect to people, particularly in blighted areas.

References

1. *Powers and Constitution of Local Councils* (Charles Arnold-Baker OBE), Introduction.
2. *People's Power* (Dr E. F. Schumacher CBE).
3. Quoted in the Arts Council's *The Idea of the Village,* written by Gillian Darley.
4. Obsolete Industrial Areas Project Report (Metropolitan Borough of Rochdale: R. B. Hargreave, Borough Planning Officer).

Worth Reading
Heritage Over the Wensum, 75p from City Planning Officer, City Hall, Norwich.

9 · RESOURCES

It must be obvious that both local and central Government are incapable of providing all the funds necessary for the maintenance of the environment, employment, housing, or social services. Although it will remain the prime provider for the foreseeable future, it must be supplemented or replaced by other action, funded and organised differently. This will be best undertaken by those most affected by the shortfall of official action – namely the local communities, particularly in areas of dereliction and blight. This chapter therefore considers how such local communities and other non-official agencies can gather sufficient resources to carry out such work. The fundamental points are these:

(a) There are some things for which society is unable to pay the full commercial cost of development, labour and materials.

(b) The time has come to break down the pattern of concentrating development in the hands of two large groupings – the local Councils and the large private developers. New agencies such as co-operatives, parish councils, conservation societies, and small groups of investors should be encouraged to take up development in a small way. The risk becomes smaller, the possible damage becomes less, and the proliferation of smaller users could lead to a greater sector of the population taking part in the development of their own area than ever before.

(c) There should be an urgent re-examination of the duties of district Councils to see whether some of the many tasks which they are currently unable to perform successfully should not be devolved upon local people.

Resources, as a term, includes money, labour, and goodwill. Goodwill includes the concept of volunteer labour, self-build and general co-operation; and the smaller the scheme, the more goodwill becomes important. This chapter deals with finance from the very small scale right up to the big business of pension funds and investment trusts, so that promoters will be able to draw on the method of fund-raising most appropriate to their particular project.

If the existing patterns of finance are no longer proving adequate, it becomes necessary to consider *all other other available sources*, no matter how risible, to see whether any of them will form an adequate substitute either individually or collectively. After all, even a risible source of finance which produces the goods is better than a deadly serious source of finance which has dried up. A good example of the type of fund-raising which has often been ridiculed is that adopted by the parishioners of All Saints Parish Church, Isleworth (London), who wished to rebuild their mediaeval and Georgian church which had been destroyed by fire during the last war. Some of the funds were raised by jumble sales, parish appeals and by the sale of some excellent home-made marmalade and jam. The parishioners earned their nice new church, passers-by bought the marmalade and the system worked (with difficulty – but it worked). What would the scoffers have – that there should be no parish church at all? In the case of the Crumbles Play Castle and the Fleet School Parents' Room, the residents and parents also earned their buildings, although in this case what they were giving was not money but labour.

Sources of Money: Grants from Official Bodies

The amount of money available from the Government and official bodies is quite staggering, and provided you are prepared to tolerate the plethora of bureaucracy the following are available for tapping:

(a) *Tourist Grants* The English Tourist Board is prepared to give loans and grants for tourist projects particularly in development areas (Development and Tourism Act 1969) and although the scale is not paricularly large with about £2 million to spend per annum, it is nevertheless significant.

(b) *Rural Industries* The Council for Small Industries in Rural Areas (COSIRA) gives loans from £100 to £20,000 over 20 years towards purchasing machinery or working capital. Apparently the term 'rural areas' can include some quite large towns.

(c) *Finance for Industry* exists specially to lend money to industry for 10–20 years with interest rates usually similar to those of clearing banks.

(d) *Clearing Banks* loan money for about 60 per cent of investment in industry at a rate of about 15 per cent for overdraft, or 18 per cent for special loans.

(e) *The Industrial Common Ownership Finance* is a revolving fund which makes loans from £500 to £10,000 at 3 per cent above bank deposit rate, specifically to assist co-ownership companies. It is unclear whether community ownership of businesses or companies would qualify for loans from this organisation.

(f) *Community Industry* is an activity usually organised by the local Council whose purpose is to help socially disadvantaged unemployed young people by providing them with realistic working experience. The youngsters work 40 hours a week; the work undertaken is usually in the nature of community projects, and all wage costs are met by the Government. In Islington, Community Industry has been going for 18 months, during which time it has undertaken 15 projects and now employs over 50 people. The project work is work that must be interesting, for the good of the community, and work that *would otherwise not get done*; the project sponsor must provide the materials. In Lewisham, Community Industry is going to convert existing drying rooms and outbuildings on the Perystreete Estate to provide a community centre, youth club and a hobbies room. The project includes landscaping the surrounding area and providing play facilities. Community Industry is operated under the auspices of the National Association of Youth Clubs, and is jointly financed by the Department of Employment and the Council.

(*g*) *Job Creation Scheme* The range of projects which can be considered for help under the job creation scheme is wide, and those that follow are merely selected examples: improvements, repair and decoration of short-life housing; initial works to empty dwellings required as part of a municipalisation programme; minor labour-intensive improvements to the urban environment and the rehabilitation of historic buildings. These may all be sponsored by local Councils as part of the job creation programme.

(*h*) *Unemployment Relief* A £1 million grant is being given to Birmingham's housing department to help alleviate unemployment in the construction industry, the money being given to firms whose contracts are about to expire, or to help create jobs for skilled craftsmen. Furthermore, the Construction Industry Training Board can give grants of up to £750 to builders who take on redundant apprentices.

(*i*) *Urban Aid* The Home Office administers grants under the urban programme (Local Government Grants [Social Need] Act 1969) which provides 75 per cent to additional expenditure incurred by local Councils in areas of special social need, 75 per cent to certain local Councils and 100 per cent to other bodies for research. For example, in 1975 the Home Office received applications for £14.4 million in urban aid grants (Phase 14 of the Urban Aid programme) as compared with the £4 million which was available. The requests for urban aid grants have to come through the local Council who can amend, or approve community schemes, or indeed put the Council's own schemes first on the list. The community and Council do not always see eye to eye as in a case in Liverpool where the local community's view was that the Council's schemes 'would employ 120 people in short term projects (recreation schemes, parks etc) whereas the community's lists of projects would have themselves created 62 full time and over 200 part time construction jobs over 5 years.' (*Community Action* 23).

(*j*) *Development Grants* Applicable in intermediate or develop-

Manpower Services commission job creation scheme where school leavers are restoring a length of the Rochdale canal. Similar work, funded by the job creation scheme, is about to start on Kennet and Avon canal.

ment areas, and consisting of: (i) A grant of 85 per cent of the net capital expenditure incurred in enabling derelict, neglected or unsightly land situated within development, intermediate or derelict land clearance areas to be brought into use or improved in appearance (Local Employment Act 1972). (ii) A grant of 50 per cent of the notional loan charges incurred in carrying out works for the reclamation or improvement of derelict, neglected or unsightly land anywhere in England and Wales (1966 Local Government Act). (iii) The Department of Trade and Industry gives regional development grants of 20 per cent of the cost of providing new buildings fully or mainly for prescribed activities. (iv) Factories may be provided for projects creating additional employment (perhaps rent-free for the first two years of occupation). (v) Loans are available on favourable terms from the Department of Trade and Industry, for projects which provide additional employment; on non-preferential terms for projects which safeguard employment when money cannot be raised elsewhere; or instead, grants can be made towards interest costs of finance provided from non-public sources for projects which provide additional employment.

If some of the above sounds confusing, the key fact to bear in mind is that there are various Government departments each one with a certain amount of money to spend, rather like a many-handed Asian goddess, and it is wise to know which particular source you wish to tap to make your application most cost-effective. In addition to some of the schemes mentioned above, the Government has a number of others also, including comprehensive community schemes and community development projects. Not all these are always greeted with enthusiasm, and the magazine *Community Action* makes a fair point, when it greeted the new comprehensive community project with this sour editorial:

'*Dab a Little CCP on it*

Another £25 million to try to find out how to solve the problems of city poverty! . . . it is amazing how easy it is for the Home Office day dreamers to pay £25 million – try getting £500 from them to help set up an action centre. How much of the £25 million will be soaked up in providing more highly paid jobs for the boys in the community work industry?'

Not all sources of Government funds are obvious, and there appears to be a whole range of what are grandly called 'Special Grants' (which usually mean grants dependent upon the whim of a Minister), such as a grant of £18,000 to the Covent Garden Community Association to convert the Shorts Gardens houses into flats.

Recycling of Money

De Gaulle is reputed to have uttered the phrase 'To govern is to choose' which, for the purposes of this chapter, is being interpreted as 'How do you spend or direct the resources which are available?' Equally, how can one make the money one has go very much further than before? For example, you can spend funds which have been raised on a straightforward capital project; or you can spend that money making more money by investment or speculation; or you can think sideways, question how the funds you hold can be supplemented by other funds, and then use them to act as pump primer. For example, the GLC is proposing to spend the sum of about £12,000 for interim environmental work in the Bermondsey Comprehensive Development Area. The way local Councils spend the money would mean the £12,000 could easily get lost on the few bits of grass (I believe that these are now known as 'amenity open spaces') and a few benches. Naturally, if the £12,000 were made available to the local organisations for materials on the grounds that they provided the labour free, such money would go very much further. Another option (still with the same amount of money) would be to set up a small organisation of one or two full-time employees who would take on youths under the job creation programme or community service volunteer programme. If this option were chosen, and the full-time worker were a gardener, instead of providing a few bits of grass, £12,000 could finance a team able to cultivate or plant many acres. In other words, £12,000 can go almost as far as a piece of string, depending on how it were used. Unfortunately, there are certain difficulties with the job creation scheme, since the employer – the full-time worker suggested above – is responsible for filling in all the burdensome employment forms, paying the necessary national insurance, taxes and so forth. This tends to have the result that many people who could take on youths under this scheme are deterred.

Take another example: the Royal Borough of Kensington and Chelsea proposes to spend £10,000 on a film illustrating the problems of North Kensington. Would it not be a greater help to North Kensington if that money were spent employing two skilled people for a year, with a team of unemployed school leavers (under the job creation scheme), to carry out direct works in the area? A recent success in recycling money in this way occurred in Pulborough (Sussex) where a road bridge collapsed into the Wey and Arun canal. The local conservation society persuaded the roads authority to give the society the money it was going to spend on filling in the canal; and the combination of this money and volunteer effort was sufficient to rebuild the original bridge and save the canal for future navigation.

A similar approach might be taken to the funds of smaller organisations. For example, many large, well-equipped schools provide carpentry, brickwork, building and ironwork classes, each of which has an annual budget. Unfortunately many such classes are ignored or poorly patronised. However, if the combined budgets and skills of these departments were added to the annual maintenance or expansion budget, together they might be sufficient to finance a new building – built by the children and supervised by their specialist teachers.

In conclusion, there are more ways of getting money than just going and asking for it.

Charities

The very word charity is coming to have a suspect meaning, in that when people use phrases like 'Well, it's only a charity' they usually mean that money from such sources is special and not significant in the world of big business. Yet charities control vast sums of money, and the funds of many are lying dormant until such time as a skilful Aladdin with the right password manages to open their caves. Most charities have a business-like purpose, and a good number are local in intention, with some widely phrased bequest such as 'To benefit the poor of Little Codling-ton'. Details of the most active charities are contained in the 'Directory of grant making Trusts' (Charities Aid Fund, 48 Pen-bury Road, Tonbridge, Kent) and some of them have been pre-pared to experiment with grants for urban research (Sainsbury Foundation). or with low-interest loans for the setting up of co-ownership building companies (The Rowntree Trust helped fund Sunderlandia, one of the first of such ventures). Occasionally, parish councils have the responsibility for adminis-tering local charities, and it would be worth approaching them to find out details of what local charities exist. Local libraries, or district Councils may be able to provide further information on the same subject.

Charities are not insignificant; they have frequently been the reverse side of capitalism (or of its unacceptable face), their total assets are enormous and the money is there to be used.

Raising Funds Locally

Local groups or communities can raise funds by means of many different fund-raising activities such as festivals, raffles, totes, sponsorship, or even tapping local businessmen or sympathetic banks. Depending upon the nature of the project for which they are raising money, they may be able to wheedle some finance from the local Council of Social Service, the Community Rela-tions Council, local Rotary clubs, Round Tables or Chambers of Commerce, local charities or even the local students' Rag week. None of these sources are to be despised as being too paltry, since funds from them could be adequate to restore a community back on to the path of self-respect in preparation for positive action; or they could be used as pump primers for raising money from other organisations.

Interest-free Money

At most times, but particularly during times of inflation, the cost of borrowing money can be crippling both to the private industry and to the authorities. For example, the chairman of the Hammerson Property Investment Trust said at a recent annual general meeting that developers such as his company, looked to making a return of about 3 per cent above the cost of money, and he was having to borrow money at a rate of 14–15 per cent. This would mean that in order to break even, developments would have to give a return of about 18 per cent, and few were doing so. (Indeed one may question whether a development providing a return of 18 per cent would be one which would be locally acceptable. Few high-profit developments in recent years have either been well designed or aimed at improving the neighbourhood in which they are situated.) Developments by non-profit-making organisations such as local communities, action groups or conservation societies therefore already have a 3–4 per cent edge on developers, and this is crucial since it could mean that a local society could take over and convert an old mill where a developer has already rejected the scheme as being uneconomic, particularly if they can get help from the agencies already mentioned which give lower interest loans to certain types of organisations.

The effect of interest rates on local Councils is probably even worse than that on private companies. The following detailed example is taken from the book *Housing Co-operatives* by John Hands. Take the total capital cost of a new house or flat as being £12,000. The Council is given authority by the Government to borrow money (say, at 15 per cent over 40 years) which gives an annual loan repayment cost of £1,806 per annum, added to a notional running cost of, say, £150 per annum. The full economic rent to pay these off would be £37.60 per week. The Exchequer gives a local Council a subsidy equal to 66 per cent of the loan charges thereby covering £22.92 per week, giving a net economic rent of £14.68 per week. It is likely that for a unit of this size (judged by cost) the rent officer or Council will fix the rent at about £7 per week; which means that for this unit, and for every other unit like it, the revenue or rates subsidy from the local authority is £7.68 per week. The accumulated figure for the country as a whole is appalling: in 1973/74, local Councils spent a total of £1,843 million in loan charges alone.

The Government Cuts – What can they cut?

The Government's only real power is that of turning off the tap, and in this context the tap refers to refusing to cover a certain amount of the Council's interest charges and cutting back on the rate-support grant. To be precise, it means that the DoE will no longer pay the subsidy for new buildings equivalent to 66 per cent of interest charges on approved costs, or to 75 per cent of the interest charges assessed over 20 years for improved houses or 90 per cent where the houses are within housing action areas or general improvement areas. The Government's control over housing associations is that it can refuse to underwrite the difference between the money received from fair rent and the total money required to pay for the capital cost of the project. Yet the Councils and housing associations are already having to find a proportion of the costs of building themselves. If the cost of interest was removed, would that not mean that Councils and housing associations could build themselves without financial dependence upon the Government? If so, how could this be done?

Raising Interest-free Money

(a) *Sinking Funds*. Those interested in history will recall that the English Government in the late seventeenth and early eighteenth century was always financially embarrassed, and from time to time attempted to set up a sinking fund. The principle is simple: save a little part of income each year and put it into the equivalent of a deposit account, thus building up enough capital reserves until such time as it is possible to use the interest to finance projects. Once the sinking fund is used whether as a revolving fund (see later) or as an immediate capital fund, all projects financed this way will not have to bear the cost of borrowing money.

Some of the sections that follow illustrate ways in which capital can be raised within the existing system to provide money for this sinking fund. However, those Councils who were going to build this year, but whose Government subsidy has been cut, might consider the following proposal: that they put into a sinking fund that amount of subsidy that they themselves would have to have met from the rates (and John Hands's example suggests something like £7.68 per dwelling unit per week), allowing that money to accumulate. For example, if a Council were planning to build 200 houses this year, at a notional cost of £15,000 each then the amount that the Council would have paid *from its own rates* for this development would have been in the region of £79,600 a year. Since that money was already allocated, the local authority could put it into a deposit account, add to it the following year, and then within three years they would have enough capital to start, albeit in a small way, building on their own, without Government fetters. This is not necessarily a matter of cheaper building or saving money, merely one of freedom from Government control.

(b) *Revolving Funds*. The principle of this method is to raise enough capital to start off with one project; then once that project has proved a success, either rent or sell the building and use the funds thus raised to carry out another. This method has been used by the National Trust for Scotland to restore a lot of houses in Fife, it is being used by Suffolk County Council to restore some cottages in Woodbridge, and it is being used by the Suffolk Preservation Society among many others. All that is required to start it off is the initial capital and this can be raised in a number of ways.

(c) *Rates*. Raising funds by rates provides the capital as suggested above. People are prepared to pay rates if they are asked to do so for specific projects for a specific period. There is great antagonism towards paying higher rates if it seems as though it will become a permanent drain upon people's personal resources. For example, Chester Council has been imposing a conservation rate of 0·8p for a number of years now and since the Government matches the money raised, this gives Chester an income of over £400,000 per annum to spend on conservation projects. The proposed scheme for the Rochdale General Improvement Area is partly financed by a levy which has been put on the rates equivalent to 1 per cent of the district's entire annual budget, specifically raised for environmental purposes, which raised over £400,000 in 1975 and matched by funds from the DoE. There have been no complaints about money being raised in this way.

(d) *Heritage and other Bonds*. Those who maintain that building houses for sale or for rent is no longer economic may be repeating a generally held theory, but one that does not equate with reality. Why else would Ladbroke's, the gambling combine, invest some £900,000 in the new housing development near Swindon? So, assuming that housing is profitable, one way of financing it is by issuing bonds. For example, Exeter City Council is considering issuing Heritage Bonds by which it hopes to raise capital to repair and convert historic buildings in Exeter. But bonds can be issued for any building, aiding local people to contribute to housing in their area by investing in it. Calculations have been worked out in some detail by James Sperling[1] which show that people who invest in bonds in building can make a substantial return, on the principle that the rate of interest on the bond itself remains constant (for example, 3 per cent) which is low in comparison to returns on bank deposit accounts, but that the value of the bond on which the interest is paid rises with the value in the housing market or inflation. Thus it is that the person investing in housing in this way never loses the value of his money. A recent example of building financed in this way can be seen from the advertisements in *The Guardian* for such bonds by the Portia Trust (which provides hostels for recently released prisoners), and which guarantees to repay the money if necessary by selling the building.

Those who consider this form of fund-raising as cloud-cuckoo-land might well consider what happens in Canada, where wealthy professionals consider it as a fairly normal proposition to invest their savings in building blocks of flats for rent or for sale. Take the following notional example (which could happen in this country): people investing money at the moment are requiring a return of at least $9\frac{1}{2}$ per cent because that is what they can receive either in building societies or in bank deposit accounts. Apply this to the capital cost of a house built for single people (providing four bedrooms with associated facilities) of about £14,000. A return of $9\frac{1}{2}$ per cent on this capital cost would be £1,320 per annum or about £25 per week. This would make the rent for each single person in this house about £6.50 per week exclusive of rates. Add 8 per cent for management and maintenance, and the resulting figure is still within normal rent levels. All we need now is some initiative!

(e) *Lotteries*. Another painless way of raising money is by lotteries, which the Government is now considering. Lotteries can raise the most fantastic sums: the Canadian Olympics received $225 million raised by lotteries. When the GLC considered the possibility of lotteries (25 May 1976) it decided to support the principle of national or regional lotteries undertaken by one authority, although the profits might be shared between several authorities in the region. The reasons for holding large lotteries are that they would be above fraud, that considerable publicity would be required to ensure adequate funds and support from the media, and that lotteries should be large enough, with sufficient prizes, to compete against other forms of gambling. A larger lottery, would also mean that adequate administrative expertise would be available. The GLC calculated that large lotteries could yield profits of more than £5–10 million per annum. Although some people believe that revenue from lotteries should be kept for arts and recreation – two forms of activity that very rarely meet their costs, much less make a profit – there is no reason why the use of lotteries could not be widened to other forms of social activity.

(f) *Tontine*. As readers of Robert Louis Stephenson's book *The Wrong Box* will know, Tontine is a method of raising capital which was frequently used when money was short, as during the Georgian period. Capital is raised from a small number of local people for the construction of a public building, from which they all share in the income according to the proportion in which they have invested. The building is then inherited by the heirs of the last member of the Tontine to die, thus avoiding death duties. Among buildings so financed was the late eighteenth-century Assembly Rooms in Glasgow.

Raising Money from Normal Sources

An obvious source of finance for house building is the Building Societies movement, and one would have thought (from their titles at least) that they would show an interest in promoting new housing development in the areas from which they originate. But it is rare for Building Societies to take a special interest in the areas whence they originated. In any case, they invest in the borrower rather than in the building, and consequently were very largely to blame for 1973 hyper-inflation in house prices, since there were plenty of people around with money to spend on houses, but insufficient new houses being built to meet this demand. Moreover, the Building Societies operate very restrictive practices regarding the types of houses on which they are prepared to advance money – it can be extremely difficult to raise finance for houses both over a certain age, or in certain districts of some towns. The Building Societies *could* finance a special agency for the purpose of constructing houses, but they have preferred instead to leave that to others and merely finance the home owners. One must presume, therefore, that unless they undergo a change of heart, they must be ignored for the time being.

Pension Funds

Pension funds and superannuation funds have at their control a quite awesome amount of money. In the past few years, such funds have invested heavily in property, a great deal of it in mammoth, poorly designed and disliked commercial developments and as a result several pension funds lost a great deal of money. Can they be persuaded to invest in other forms of development as well as these large commercial developments?

Firstly, if mixed developments on the co-operative principle were proposed whereby houses, commercial developments, shops, hotels and so on were all part of the same package, the rate of return might be sufficient to gain the pension funds' backing. After all, a certain amount of discretion is permitted in how pension fund money is spent, as witness an announcement in the papers that the South Yorkshire County Council was proposing to invest a certain proportion of its pension fund in local businesses. If they can invest in local businesses they can invest in other things, such as housing.

Pension funds require the same return from all long-term investment, be they gilts, equities or property. A fund decides at the time it has money to invest which avenue is likely to have the most attractions and, generally speaking, the funds will aim for investments which will give a return of at least the same amount as can be achieved on gilt-edged stocks whose yield is guaranteed by the Government. Take, for example, the yield on gilt-edged currently at 14 per cent. There are various ways in which the yield on other investments can be calculated to produce a return of 14 per cent. For example, the massive pension fund investment in agricultural land over the last ten years, has produced an estimated capital growth of approximately 10 per cent per annum, compounded, to which should be added a yield of about 4 per cent by way of rent, giving a total growth of 14 per cent, the same as that obtained on gilts. It has already been demonstrated earlier in this chapter that investment in housing could probably make a return of $9\frac{1}{2}$ per cent; if one added to that investment the so-called 10 per cent compounded as being the capital growth of bricks and mortar, one could argue that investment in housing could produce a total return of 19–20 per cent. The question of rent control, and security of tenure is discussed in the next chapter; but it should be noted that there are methods both within existing legislation and in possible new legislation which would give pension funds adequate control to ensure that investment in housing for rent or for sale would provide a return as great as that in some other forms of investment.

The splendid Camden Lock scheme in London, where canalside buildings have been taken over by craft shops and studios, restaurants, a market and similar activities. It is now firmly part of the tourist circuit. It is also under threat of imminent redevelopment.

Co-operative Schemes

One way of achieving results is to approach projects co-operatively, uniting different sectors of society to common ends. What follows are a few examples of how results are achieved without the obvious money being available. The first example is that of a block of magnificent early eighteenth-century almshouses in Bow, London, called the Drapers Almshouses, owned by the GLC and neglected and decaying for many years. The GLC is now offering these almshouses at a peppercorn rent to anybody prepared to take on the building and restore it to the GLC's own specification. The restorer will have a 99-year lease in return for his work. A different example is that of a hotel in Carmarthen, which recently decided to pay from its own funds for the restoration of the Roman amphitheatre. The reason for so doing, was that it would increase the tourist potential of Carmarthen and therefore presumably bring more people to the hotel. Another example of thinking sideways, is that of the Guardian

Housing Association, which persuades elderly people to sell their large houses, and with the proceeds buy a life interest in a flat with the Guardian Housing Association. When the residents die, the flat reverts to the Housing Association. A further example of sharing aims and resources, is derived from the GLC minutes (25th May 1976). It appears that the main brewery companies trading in the Greater London area are willing to provide financial assistance and other help to private clubs usually based on the anticipated sale of the company's products. Such help can take the form of a non-repayable, interest-free loan written off at so much a barrel; larger interest-free loans repayable over an agreed period, or a loan of a much larger sum at a low interest rate repayable over several years. These arrangements are generally used for working men's clubs and institutes.

In the joint venture for the Colegate Area in Norwich, already discussed in Chapter 8, the City Council joined together with a group of private individuals and bodies to promote the revival of this district. The Council and a local developer (R. G. Carter Limited) set up a new joint company – Colegate Developments Limited – whose purpose was to produce the new housing on Friar's Quay; and the Council and the Norwich Society jointly set up the Norwich Preservation Trust which undertook the restoration of some old buildings and the construction of some new ones. The joint venture was considered beneficial to the Council in that it enabled the Council to borrow money from the City, and to the company because it avoided Corporation Tax and Income Tax. Most towns of reasonable size have a major developer, and it could well be that joint ventures of this sort could be repeated throughout the United Kingdom.

If the recommendations in this book are followed, you have found the land, you have found the money; so what remains to be sorted out before local communities and groups can start working? That is discussed in the next chapter.

References
1. *Living Over the Shop*, RIBA Eastern Region, 75p.

Books
Forming a Buildings Preservation Trust, Civic Trust, 60p.

10 · WHAT CHANGES ARE REQUIRED?

Some significant changes in both local Government and Council attitudes are required if the trend towards community-based development is to be consolidated, or if local communities are to supplement or replace some local authority activity. The changes required fall into two distinct categories – the first is a change in *policy direction*; and the second is a change in the methods by which Councils and their servants carry out their statutory tasks, of planning, grant administration, land allocation and enforcement of standards.

A change of policy direction is required regarding the use of derelict land for as long as the owner has no use for it, and the following simple principles are ones which any Council or authority interested in the conservation of resources would probably be glad to support.

(*a*) No virgin land should be built over, or sound building demolished whilst there exists in the area of the proposal derelict land which could be used instead.

(*b*) No building should remain empty where there is a responsible application for its use.

(*c*) Where there is a proposal by local organisations for the interim use of derelict land, there should be a presumption in favour of permitting the proposal.

(*d*) There should also be a presumption in favour of permitting tenants to undertake the maintenance and improvement of their own estates, and allocating to such tenants the normal funds which are set aside for this purpose.

(*e*) Where land is in the ownership of the Council, the Council should be obliged to state the minimum period of time that the land is likely to remain derelict, and to permit the use of that land for that period by local organisations.

(*f*) Those wishing to use a property responsibly must be given every assistance to do so.

(*g*) The principle of mixed use for both buildings and areas should be a prime objective.

These proposals are all based on the presumption that local groups or organisations – and particularly parish or community councils – are or can be made responsible bodies and able to take over certain functions in their own area.

Devolution of Planning Powers

Responsible parish councils, which already have the right to vet planning applications, could take on much of the decision-making function from the existing district Councils, particularly where small-scale problems are involved.

Current legislation permits householders (under the General Development Order – GDO) to carry out works of a certain scale to their own houses without permission. The good point about the GDO is that it still permits a small amount of freedom to the individual. The bad feature is that if there is a dispute with neighbours, it usually has to be settled often at considerable cost in the courts. It would be much fairer if a development (housing extension, garage, gazebo or whatever) is discussed with the neighbours and the parish council before construction is commenced. If there is no dispute then permission should be automatic. If a dispute arises, then the district Council with its professional staff should be called in as arbitrators between the disputing parties. The current exercise of planning powers by the district Council ignores not only traditional rights, but also the value of neighbourly control – after all, people have to live with neighbours. This simple reform would prevent the following case, which occurred recently in Hampstead Garden Suburb, from recurring. This concerned a small house extension to which the neighbours, and the Hampstead Garden Suburb Trust both agreed, but which Barnet Council refused. The extension could not be seen from the road, and one must presume that a body with a title like the 'Hampstead Garden Suburb Trust' takes its trust seriously, and does not agree to extensions without careful thought. So why should the Planning Act permit Barnet Council

THE GLC HAVE JUST PRODUCED THEIR LATEST PLAN FOR COVENT GARDEN. IT IS THEIR THIRD TRY IN THE LAST TEN YEARS. ALL THIS PLANNING HAS COST THE PUBLIC ABOUT £6 million. THEIR LATEST PROPOSALS ARE ALMOST AS DESTRUCTIVE AS THEIR PREVIOUS EFFORTS.

Broadsheet from the Covent Garden Community Association.

to refuse the householder to build this extension? Pleading the public good is one thing, but to plead the public good in this case clearly implies that Hampstead Garden Suburb Trust did not protect the good of the suburb adequately.

The argument against local people deciding such matters has been that they can be unduly influenced, and that the district Council can be more objective. There have been many recent, infamous cases which have shown the extent to which district and county Councils *can* be influenced, and indeed there is more scope for massive 'influence' at Council level with high expenditure rates, than there would be at a more local level. *If local people are deemed responsible enough to vote at elections and in referenda, they must surely be responsible enough to determine, without going to a higher or more distant authority, whether a neighbour's extension is acceptable?*

Local people should also have the power to accept or refuse new, small-scale businesses and industries. The key is small-scale; for the time being this could be arbitrarily fixed at the scale of development which is 'permitted development', under the Community Land Act. Planners seem to have forgotten that towns and cities grew organically, and that the great factor in the growth was the germination of large numbers of small businesses whose inventors beavered away in cramped quarters making the best of their opportunities. Planning decisions, particularly over the rate of redevelopment and zoning, have had the effect of cutting off the compost, and preventing the germination of new businesses (and it is this which the Clerkenwell Workshops hopes to solve). But if local people had the power of deciding on the normal, common-law grounds of noise, smell and disturbance, whether or not new businesses should be permitted, then their germination might begin again. The restriction by scale is necessary since it is likely that the larger businesses will have larger requirements – such as heavy lorries – and it is strategic authorities such as the district or county Councils which should deal with such matters. The difference is this: small-scale applications are likely to affect only the one locality whereas the larger ones will probably affect a number of localities. The usefulness of the district or county Council is best employed in the latter case.

Planning legislation and its operation is falling into disrepute and much of this can be attributed to the remoteness of the planners. Witness the case of a farmer who, instructed to paint his buildings a certain colour, threatened to cut down all the trees on his land and paint all his buildings orange. As it happens, the Council did not have the power to thus instruct the farmer, so the latter kept the buildings he wanted and left his trees standing. A similar case occurred in Derbyshire where a tourist attraction was refused permission to erect a gigantic flagpole. On the day of the enquiry, all the householders from the town erected flagpoles in their gardens and flew the Union Jack, as a way of informing those distant officials that, as far as they were concerned, the tourist attraction was welcome to its flagpole.

In their attempts to replace discretion with rules, planners have produced policy guides and development criteria. One such Council is Stroud District Council which sternly instructs its ratepayers, developers and householders 'Never introduce false architectural features for embellishment' in a new package of design notes. The illustration to accompany these notes shows a fun house of a great deal more interest than the normal boring semi-detached: William Beckford would never have been able to build such follies as Fonthill Abbey in the territory of the modern Stroud District Council.

Public Participation

Current procedures of public participation (whereby once a planning application has been lodged, parish councils, amenity societies and other groups are consulted and a fixed length of time is provided for consultation) are not only inadequate, but tend to waste time. Applications affect a given neighbourhood in four main ways – their scale, their effect in terms of displacement of existing businesses, their use and their appearance. Matters of use and effect should be settled during the very first stages of an application, and do not need to wait for the complete design before the public is consulted. Next comes question of scale, perhaps best evaluated from a model or drawing, and finally there is the matter of its appearance. To have a public enquiry at the end of perhaps two years planning and design at which fundamental matters such as the use of the building are still being discussed – and mixed with finicky details of its final appearance – presents a travesty of public participation, and a phenomenal waste of public money. Only too often, the first time the designer of a scheme meets the local people and organisations is when he is sitting on the opposing side during a public enquiry.

In order to participate effectively, local people and organisations must have adequate access to fully qualified professionals who would be able to explain the ramifications of any scheme. Public participation could otherwise become a travesty.

A far better method of ordering matters would be to arrange that the designers of new proposals should make contact with local organisations from the very outset, so that they may assess the character of the area and how the locals see it. Matters of use and effect should be decided at an early stage by consultation between the borough Council and local people, and decisions would be taken at that stage which would be held henceforth. If this procedure were followed through all stages of scale and

'Never introduce false architectural features for embellishment.' Illustration from a package of design notes from the Local Plans Section, Stroud District Council.

design, then the consultation period, provided once the application has been submitted, can be dispensed with. The result may well be a series of compromises instead of a series of pitched battles, but only rarely do pitched battles produce decisive winners: indeed, in planning battles, the winners are usually the lawyers. This would not necessarily remove all conflict between large development proposals and local groups, but it would go a long way to remove the perpetual feelings of distrust.

Sharing Resources

The official mind thinks in furrows, and rarely realises that all furrows are together in the same field. Thus it is that a number of activities such as nurseries, primary schools, secondary schools, houses, clinics and colleges, are required to have land around them; but each wants its own land and jealously guards it against the encroachment of other uses. It is only recently that a pioneering housing scheme was acclaimed for being able to combine some school land with some housing land to produce a village green and, in order to achieve this, the designers had to go through a farrago of committees each of which had the right to decide on the future of its own patch. The resulting scheme has some excellent features, since the combined land makes a pleasant, large green area which is rare in London housing schemes. But how often is the contrary to be seen – small nursery schools surrounded by a statutory bit of land which is wired-off even from the kids themselves, overlooked by densely packed houses with tiny gardens whose occupants would dearly love to be able to sit out in the nursery school grounds on weekends when no one else is using them. The most effective way to achieve co-operation would probably be influence at local parish council level where knowledge of local conditions would be considerable. If the combined approach suggested above were adopted, it would bring the communities together and also help towards a sharing of resources.

Private Rented Accommodation

There are opportunities for local communities or parish councils to help to provide a greater supply of private rented accommodation than currently exists. The problem of private rented accommodation should be considered firstly within existing legislation, and secondly with reference to possible new legislation. Landlords are normally worried that if they rent out their premises they will not receive an adequate return (insufficient to cover repair and maintenance); but perhaps the greater fear is that of not being able to evict a tenant who proves unsuitable or who is occupying premises which the landlord wishes to repossess. If these two problems could be solved then there is a considerable chance that flats which have been withdrawn for decades would come back onto the market, which could both lower the rental of other accommodation, and help reverse the decay of residential premises which exist above shops.

The question of both rental and repossession can be solved in the same way: that is for the local district Council, or a housing association, or a reputable local organisation – such as a parish council or amenity group – to take over the lease of the property and then sub-let to other people. The organisation which takes over the lease would undertake not only to cover all repairs and maintenance save for the outside structure, but also to evict the tenants if either the tenant proved unsuitable, or the landlord had good reason to repossess. The organisation which takes on the lease can of course charge whichever rent it likes, either the full rent for the property, or a subsidised rent (as may be the case for the housing association). Councils themselves have greater powers than other organisations of eviction in case of problems. If sufficient accommodation were taken over in this way, and a landlord did wish to repossess, it would generally be possible for the local Council or the other local organisations to find alternative accommodation. It could even be that the landlord himself will be a member of the local organisation, which will merely increase his security. If a local organisation is running its own housing association as well, then this would be the ideal management organisation to take on such lettings.

For new legislation to be acceptable to all political parties, all existing privately rented accommodation must be protected. However, all such accommodation should by now be registered with the local rent officer and new legislation could specifically refer to non-registered rented accommodation, which is not at present on the market. Consequently, if new legislation were introduced which relaxed both the rent controls and security controls for new accommodation, much accommodation which had been withdrawn from the market might become available once more.

Housing Associations

Housing Associations offer the opportunity to local groups to provide homes for their members; but unfortunately the bureaucracy of the Housing Corporation (the Housing Association's financial overlord) is frustrating this. The Corporation has ceased to register new Housing Associations, maintaining that people with projects should approach existing associations, and this has led to some Councils to zone their territories for selected Associations. The example of the Soho Association (Chapter 7) illustrates that such a policy will remove the local touch which is so necessary. Indeed, had the Soho Association been founded now, it would probably have had to be joined to the Paddington Churches Association – a good distance away, and already so large that it is having considerable problems with the maintenance of its dwellings. Local groups therefore must pressure the Housing Association zoned for their area to divide its programme into local projects, planned and supervised by local people following the example of the Community Housing Association (Chapter 6). The original purpose of Housing Associations was to circumvent bureaucracy, not to increase it.

Do we really need standards?

It is only when ordinary people have to take to building or converting their own houses themselves that it is realised the extent to which new standards of building construction have been imposed over the last few years, with the consequent considerable rise in the cost of building. Since the building professionals have dealt mainly with large clients, it has been possible for the Government to impose more and more stringent rules and regulations without any backlash. Those days are over. Now that more work is to be done by local Councils and individuals who do not have unlimited funds, much greater flexibility will have to be applied – particularly where local people are making choices for themselves.

Planning Standards

A proposal to convert a chapel into a house in a residential area was recently refused planning permission by the North Kesteven District Council on the grounds that the size and the shape of the site would not permit an adequate garden. Surely the occupier would have been well aware of the size of the garden, and had taken that into account when he made his choice to live in the chapel? It is quite possible that the occupier did not wish to have a large garden. In any case, what right has the local Council to instruct people in the size of gardens they should have?

Local Authority Residential Standards

Standards currently being enforced need re-examining because research is showing that the official standards are not always in line with those held by ordinary people. For example, politicians are fond of bandying around statistics about the housing problem by reference to the lack of an indoor lavatory. Often indeed, when Medical Officers of Health come to recommend that a house be presented as unfit, they are doing so according to a predetermined list of similar standards. But the 1975 Annual Report of the Building Research Establishment demonstrates that for ordinary people an electric light in each room, and adequate refuse collection came far higher in the ratings than did the provision of an indoor lavatory. This gives rise to a dilemma as the following quotation illustrates.

'Should house improvements be regarded as a necessary part of the good management of a long term capital asset, even though this might be contrary to the short term wishes of the current residents who might be quite happy with low standards or unable to afford the new high rents?'[1]

The point in question is whether owner-occupiers or tenants should be compelled to have their houses rehabilitated in general improvement areas if this puts the rent up to levels which they can no longer afford, particularly if they are quite happy living in existing conditions.

Only if standards are relaxed will British people be able once more to build houses in rough and ready materials as they once did. Many of the lovely half-timbered cottages throughout the country, dating from the seventeenth century or earlier, are squatter homes built under the old rule permitting building on common land if the main structure could be erected between sunrise and sunset. All over the world, squatter housing is still being built by those who cannot afford traditional methods, and frequently the materials used are those nearest to hand – rubbish, bits of this and that, wood, corrugated sheeting and the like. It was to explore whether these methods had more formal application that Martin Pawley investigated the concept of garbage hous-

ing (see Chapter 5). Indeed, it would be interesting if the producers of the most common types of cheap materials such as corrugated sheeting, could produce it in such a way that it could be easily clipped together and used for building. As can be seen in Pawley's book,[2] Heineken have already been persuaded to bottle their lager in square bottles which can be used for building afterwards. The trouble with using bottles is twofold: (a) they chip; and (b) there is usually a returnable deposit on them and the instant cash of the return deposit is more favoured than re-using the bottles for other purposes.

The conversion of old buildings can run into trouble when faced with currently enforced standards. For instance, on behalf of us all, it has been imposed that there should be a certain window-to-wall ratio to ensure that each room should get adequate light. As a rule of thumb, most buildings built before 1700 and poor buildings built before 1850, have a totally inadequate window-to-wall ratio, but this does not seem to prevent wealthy people who can afford to buy better enjoying living in them! Equally, new buildings have to have ceiling heights of 7 ft 6 in, and there are cases where existing and elderly buildings have to have their floors dug down and their roofs raised in order to provide the necessary 7 ft 6 in ceiling height. These conditions are rubbish. Many ancient Tudor houses and old picturesque pubs all have ceiling heights of less than 7 ft 6 in and nobody complains. Instead of legislating, it would be much better if the standards were put as recommendations, and where the owner is building for himself *he is able to choose*. Mike Franks, and other converters of warehouses (Chapter 5) all encountered considerable difficulties with regulations, and the Brunel Project newsletter puts the matter simply:

'Voluntary effort has a role to play in the conservation of our heritage, but it can only play its part if the statutory authorities make life considerably easier. It is surely a waste when so much professional and voluntary time, not to mention the time of all the officers who administer the regulations and grants, is taken up with negotiation, when available funds should be going on design, bricks and mortar . . . building the original tunnel is beginning to look quite straightforward compared with what happens when one tries to improve today's environment.'[3]

An interesting case occurred in California, in which the Governor and the State Architect supported a group of do-it-yourself house builders against a Chief Building Inspector. The case concerned the lack of indoor plumbing in a community of some 290 houses, and the Building Inspector demanded the demolition of the houses as a health menace. In return, the owners demanded that the state relax its stiff building codes, and the Governor said 'The philosophy of this administration is to use government to help people to help themselves. People can do a lot more for themselves than they realize.' The State Architect, Sim van der Ryn, believed that 'The answer for low cost housing is to make a break with a standard of living which makes us slaves to centralized decision making and control.' Three of the house builders have been taken to court so far, two of whom have been acquitted by the juries with a divided jury on the third. Thus a precedent may have been set for future relaxation.

Criticism can also be made of the authorities' adherence to minimum space standards regardless of other factors such as people wanting to start with a small building and add to it as circumstances permit. A marvellous case-study of a self-built house, erected in the 'thirties, which would never be allowed today is contained in the *Bulletin of Environmental Education* (August–September 1976).

Road Standards

Councils impose upon new developments what they call 'adoption standards' to which the schemes have to adhere if the Council is to undertake lighting, street cleaning and refuse collection. Usually these standards are wasteful of space and lead to the terrible 'prairie planning' of modern housing estates; and yet developers are fearful in case the Council refuses to adopt the roads. Is it not time that we should question whether we want the Council to adopt the road at all? Take this example from Wimbledon: residents facing a non-adopted road recently asked the Council if it would provide a pavement along one side, so that pedestrians could avoid the puddles in winter. The machinery ground slowly, and the residents now find that their little, rural road is tarmac, with concrete kerbs, and a pavements on *both* sides of the road: all, or nothing.

It is the same attitude which demands that by-passes must be expensive two-lane dual carriageways with hard shoulder constructions, which makes them impossibly expensive for small communities. If the local people could designate a 'heavy lorry route' instead – as they do in France – it might not be perfect, but with a bit of making-and-do, it might work better than having the traffic thundering down the high street.

The Operation of Grants

Insistence on regulations and form-filling is having a serious effect on the rehabilitation programme, and has led to a significant downturn in the application for grants, probably from those who need them most, since it is presumed that the variety of grants and the way in which they are administered has led to the more poorly educated giving up the attempt to find a way through the maze.

Grants are awarded according to criteria drawn up by the Government, and can either be *standard*, a fixed sum for a specified list of works which the Council is obliged to award if the conditions are right; or *discretionary*, which offers more money; but the award is within the Council's discretion, and the property for which the grant is being sought will have to be brought up to full standard according to local bye-laws. Since the level of grant has fallen far behind the rise in building costs, most owner-occupiers have preferred to head for discretionary grants, and the applications for standard grants in 1973 had fallen by almost 50 per cent from the 1969 figure.

However, the operation of discretionary grants can impose considerable strain on the owner-occupier, since many Councils will only pay up to 50 per cent of the grant during construction, paying the remainder after completion. This leaves the owner with the job of raising money to pay the contractor during the latter part of the contract. Furthermore, some Councils operate their discretionary grant in such a way as to make it almost less expensive for the owner *not* to apply for grants in the first place. For example, in a recent case in South London, the 'all or nothing' approach of the Council meant that although all the essentials of the house had been finished (roof, damp-proofing, plumbing, draining, electrics, bathrooms and separate front doors) the Council was able to enforce the completion of less essential items such as railings, balconies, double motor fans in the WC's, by the threat of demanding the return of all the grant money already paid, plus interest, unless such items were included.

It would be more helpful if Councils divided their discretionary grants into money for specific items, and when those items were complete, pay the money. In this way, a house could be completed over a period of years as the incomes of occupiers provided. Current methods merely put occupiers into debt, and scare other people who were considering whether to tackle the same job. The declining level of grant applications, which illustrates this point clearly, probably means that vast numbers of houses are deteriorating each year which could be saved were the bureaucracy more sympathetically organised. To quote the Brunel newsletter once more:

'Though we were helped by generous grants from a number of bodies many of the grants can only be paid after the work has been done, creating a problem of working capital. It would be far easier, and in the end far more efficient, if bodies were to give grants outright by leaving a project to decide how they should be spent.'

David Crease, Chief Architect of the York University Design Unit, writing in *Living Over the Shop* about delays experienced in converting premises above a shop into residential accommodation, points out that delays of some seven months added 11 per cent of the capital cost of the project, concluding:

'Of course it is necessary to have an official scrutiny of building costs where public money is concerned, but in this case the community has plainly lost more in cash than it has gained in a certainty of honest dealing.'[4]

Temporary Uses

As more and more land scheduled for some long-term use becomes derelict, it is ironic that Councils have become increasingly unable to deal with short-term, interim uses. Some Councils are exceptional, and Camden Council has a policy of licensing buildings for short-life accommodation or other uses. If the users prove responsible, and demonstrate that they are fulfilling a need, then they stand a good chance of having their tenancy made permanent.

The existing Building Codes may be relaxed for constructions permitted under short-term licences, and often this is the only way whereby experimental structures can be built. Both the Fleet School building, and Crumbles playcastle (and probably the GLC's many mobile homes) are on three-year licences, although in time, they may become permanent fixtures. A peculiar advantage of the Fleet School extension is that by the nature of its construction it is demountable (as will be Walter Segal's houses in Lewisham); such buildings could be constructed on unused land, then dismantled when the owner wishes to develop, and moved to the next unused site and re-erected again.

Political considerations should not blind Councils or local people to the fact that squatters often repair and maintain the derelict house which they occupy, and occasionally they behave less

The same house restored into five flats by the Covent Garden Community Association, housing 16 people at a conversion cost of only £1,150 per person. The GLC still plans to demolish in five years.

destructively than the Councils which try to evict them. Obviously this is not always the case, but press coverage is usually concentrated on the bad examples. Some Councils have begun to harness the undoubted positive energies of some squatters by licensing them, and over 60 groups are already licensed by the GLC. This is a trend that could be encouraged but might be better done at a more local level. Much of the opposition to squatters derives from the fact that they usually have few local roots and have the image of moving from district to district like an army of ants. But all squatters must originate from some locality, and if the local community have the power to lease empty local buildings to house its own homeless (or who it will) then local opposition to squatters might diminish.

House in Shorts Gardens, under threat of demolition by the GLC, and derelict for some years.

The recommendation is not so much that squatters should be officially recognised, as that Councils should understand the need to put accommodation to use even if it has only a short future life. As the examples from Blawhurst and Unipol have shown (see Chapter 6) a converted house can pay for itself within three or four years. It would be ridiculous for the Council's officials to insist that conversions of these short-life properties come up to the full standard required for houses with an indefinite life. The Covent Garden Community Association, with their creation of five flats from three derelict houses in Shorts Gardens have produced, for the total cost of £18,000, homes for 16 otherwise homeless people for five years. Now, if the Government totted up the cost of those sixteen people going into bed and breakfast accommodation for five years, and added a notional cost to cover the misery that would be caused, it is certain that the conversion in Shorts Gardens would prove to be a bargain. The Chairwoman of the GLC's Covent Garden committee made the point that 'of course the flats don't come up to GLC standards' (*Architect's Journal*, 1st August 1976): perhaps the GLC's standards are far too high for accommodation such as this – perhaps even they are, in themselves, contributing to homelessness?

References

1. Review by Christopher Barnes (in *Planning*) of J. Trevor Robert's Book *General Improvement Areas*.
2. Martin Pawley, *Garbage Housing*, Architectural Press 1974.
3. Brunel Project/Rotherhithe: Newsletter 8.
4. *Living Over the Shop*, RIBA Eastern Region (edited by Charles McKean), 75p from RIBA, 66 Portland Place, London WIN 4AD.

Of interest

Architectural Design, August 1976.
Housing Improvement Handbook – self-help for resident groups (available from J. Bloor, 9 Queenston Road, Manchester 20).
Unpublished paper by Charles McKean for RIBA Eastern Region on Private Rented Accommodation.
Evidence submitted to House of Commons Expenditure Committee – environmental sub-committee on planning delays – by the RIBA London Environment Group.

11 · PROFESSIONAL ADVICE FOR THE PUBLIC

A project undertaken by local people or groups need be no less skilful, beautiful or effective than those undertaken by large-scale organisations such as Councils or the Government. Indeed, providing that the right skills are available, there is a strong chance that such projects will be as good, *if not better*, than official projects. The key lies in the question of advice. As has been seen, a skilful mural is more effective than a poorly executed mural – and although residents and local people helped paint the Floyd Road mural (Greenwich) they were led, helped and co-ordinated by skilled artists from the Greenwich Mural Workshop, supported with grants from the Greater London Arts Association. Projects like the Crumbles Castle, Fleet School or ASSIST all had architects or planners intimately concerned: Mike Franks in Clerkenwell is an ex-architect; Jim Monahan of Covent Garden trained as an architect; Dickon and Charlotte Robinson from Soho are both architects; Chris Whittaker is an architect planner; NUBS has an architect Director; Keith Cheng (who designed the Japanese Flower Garden) is an architect; the '20 Ideas for Bristol' exhibition was partly organised by architects; Rod Hackney is an architect – and so on. Some of the advice which the professionals have given has been free of charge (offered in their capacity as members of the community); and some has been on a full professional basis. But little doubt exists that if greater power is to be devolved to more local levels, then full professional advice – however paid – must be made available.

Professional advice is equally important at public enquiries. Chris Whittaker points out that at Compulsory Purchase

Is change necessarily a change for the better?

Enquiries the Councils put forward a highly professional team often including the Medical Officer of Health, the Architect, the Surveyor, the Planner and sundry other officials, all represented by a solicitor, and a barrister with his junior. Facing these heavyweights, is Mrs Bloggs, often a poor owner-occupier, possibly a widow. According to his terms of reference, the inspector us expected to make a decision on evidence as submitted and he too is a professional. Quite patently, the chances of a fair balance between the two parties to produce fair hearing is remote.

Moreover, there is evidence that some Councils dislike anybody who dares to oppose them:

'"I'm scared of the Council," said the woman who lives near Camberwell Green in the London Borough of Southwark, "they're so vindictive." Anonymous because of her fear, she survives on tranquillisers having at last realised her symptoms of physical disease relate rather to the threat of the bulldozers, forced removal from her home, and the unlikelihood of compensation enabling the family to buy the equivalent accommodation in an equivalent neighbourhood with equal access to bus routes, work, shops and schools.

Such, sadly, is the usual atmosphere of an area still unnecessarily scheduled for redevelopment – the local people regarding the town hall as some kind of tyranny which cannot be changed because the ruling party has such a huge majority it will never be voted out of power.' (Judy Hillman, *The Guardian*, 12 April 1976)

At a recent enquiry into a town centre redevelopment with the consequent closure of ancient rights of way, a Council in the north of England applied to the Secretary of State to have costs of some £15,000 to be awarded *against* the objectors, on the grounds that the objections were vexatious and put up as delaying tactics. Some people saw this as yet another attempt into terrorising the public into not objecting in the future, and the Secretary of State's decision has been greeted with relief:

'As a general principle, objectors should not be liable to pay costs. This is so persons can put forward their objections without fear of financial loss should their objections be found to be without foundation. To place inhibitions in the path of persons wishing to express opinions could seriously detract from the effectiveness of democratic planning procedures.'

But the democracy of planning enquiries is not greatly in evidence, and so Whittaker and a number of other planners, and also Town and Country Planning Association, have been investigating and developing the concept of *planning aid*. If Councils put forward proposals partial to their point of view, local people have only the public enquiry and the appeals procedure on which to depend, if some impartial judgement in the circumstance is to be made; and the Planning Aid scheme, therefore, is one whereby objectors at such enquiries could be provided with full professional planning advice, if necessary free of charge, in the identical way to the availability of legal advice in the courts. Only in this way can a balance at the enquiry be achieved, and the Council's proposals adequately questioned.

Rod Hackney concluded that, at Black Road, Macclesfield, 'the presence of a qualified person (as referred to in circular 65/69 from the Ministry of Housing and Local Government) was of immeasurable value when it came to negotiations with the Council and later the contractors. There is therefore an argument here for calling for professional residents in future areas of general improvement or housing action. That is people willing to give all their time to helping implement the housing improvement programme.' Although there are certain pressure groups – such as the Architects Revolutionary Council, and the New Architecture Movement, together with a group of students from the Architectural Association – which give advice to certain local communities on certain specific problems, this is a far cry from the community-based approach which Hackney recommends. Some advice is available from such bodies as Citizens Advice Bureaux; and both the Royal Institute of British Architects (RIBA) and the Royal Town Planning Institute (RTPI) are considering setting up planning aid and architectural advice schemes; and members of their local branches occasionally give advice through Citizens Advice Bureaux. The Town and Country Planning Association has a full-time planning aid officer, and help is available from organisations such as Shelter and Legal Advice Centres.

It is not clear from where money to pay for such professional advice will be coming. The Covent Garden Community Association received a grant for professional salaries from the Monument

The 'London for the People' demonstration marching into Trafalgar Square. Marching is all very well, but that same energy could be channelled into more positive works.

Trust; ASSIST in Glasgow received grants from Urban Aid, the City Council, and others. Certainly, if outside consultants are to be employed and paid, then some of the sources of finance mentioned in the previous chapter may help to foot the bill. But this can be very expensive as the objectors at the M3 Enquiry in Winchester and those at the Liverpool Street Station Enquiry in London have discovered to their great cost. It would be fair if a restriction were placed upon the promoters (in this case the Government and British Rail) as to how much money *they* could spend at such enquiries.

Professional aid to the public requires a great deal of commitment, although it is unlikely that this will reach the level of commitment provided by ARAU (Atelier de Recherche et d'Actions Urbaines) in Brussels. There the objective is to democratise the decision-making process, and this is done by holding monthly press conferences and presenting counter-proposals for various planning applications. ARAU consider that 'one of the conditions for democratic town planning consists in the possibility of comparing different options'.[1] That seems to be a suitable note on which to end.

Reference

1. *Architectural Association Quarterly,* Vol. 7, No. 4.

Of interest

1. *Handbook of Environmental Powers*, Chris Whittaker, Jane Monahan, Peter Brown; Architectural Press, £8.95.

12 · CONCLUSIONS

At the beginning of this book, it was questioned whether the Council 'machine' was stopping, unable to cope with the demands put upon it; and whether more local organisations could supplement or take over some of the Councils' functions. If this were to happen, local organisations would have to prove their capability and their responsibility.

The examples in the book demonstrate that local organisations *do* have both the capability and responsibility that is required; they also demonstrate that the Councils *are* unable to cope with everything required of them, primarily because of their size and remoteness, and particularly since local Government reorganisation combined them into larger units.

These Councils need to have some of their powers devolved to smaller groupings – such as parish councils (in rural areas) and community councils (in towns and cities). If this happened, the existing large Councils (borough or district Councils) should change their function from that of dictating from the top, to that of helping, financing, and advising the local people to take their own action.

For local action to be fully effective, local professional expertise should be exploited fully, particularly that of architects, planners, surveyors, illustrators and painters; conversely, the more community-based such professionals become, the better the result is likely to be. Everyone knows the village doctor; but is it not time we began to hear about the village architect or the village painter? The purpose of involving the professionals is not so much getting *them* to do the work, as getting them to help ordinary people to do it, thus releasing and encouraging people's creativity. It is not enough merely to build a structure (such as the

Crumbles Castle) in an arid environment and simply leave it; a creative atmosphere has to be encouraged as well.

In the meantime, the blight has to be tackled, almost in the manner of a Mrs Beaton recipe: first, find your land and negotiate its use; then carry out temporary works to restore morale in the locality (such as murals, painting, festivals or gardens); then proceed to longer term projects, such as city farms, co-operative warehouses, or establishing community centres; and finally, build (or rehabilitate) for yourself.

This is not a recipe for an easy or a popular life. It will mean spending a great deal of spare time on community activities which could be spent otherwise; it could also involve heavy manual work. It is likely to mean *participation* by everyone in the community – including the shy and the anti-social. But the result will be an environment of your own choosing, maintained to your own standards and controlled by you. For communities currently blighted, the message is clear: stop waiting for the Council to do something and do it yourselves.

As the founder of the Garden Cities Movement, Ebenezer Howard, said to Sir Frederick Osborne: 'My dear fellow, if you wait for the Government to act, you'll be as old as Methuselah before they start. *The only way to get anything done is to do it yourself.'*

POSTSCRIPT AND CASE STUDIES

Introduction

Since the completion of the main part of this book (August 1976) and now (February 1977) the politicians have realised that inner city dereliction could become vote catching, and contrive therefore to mention it about once a week. Another of the Home Office's 'Inner urban studies', this time dealing with Stockwell, (south west London), has been published. Predictably, it revealed a poor environment, some social conflict, and poverty, concluding (equally predictably) that massive injections of Government funds were required both to help the existing inhabitants to leave and to improve the area. Such conclusions are not new; equally, they are not realistic. Conditions in Stockwell are probably no worse than conditions in thousands of similar areas, and Government funds are simply not available on the scale this report seems to suggest as necessary. Moreover, the report fails to see that the question of how the money is spent, *and by whom*, is just as important as making the money available in the first place. For similar reasons, some scepticism of the politicians' statements may be justified; and will continue to be justified until it is made more clear how much money is available, and to whom it will be given to spend. It may well be that the cost effectiveness of each £1 spent in a Walter Segal scheme, or in a Rod Hackney or Chris Whittaker rehabilitation is far greater than that of each £1 given to Housing Associations or to local Authorities.

This is the crunch point: as the country runs out of money, how can we achieve *more* with *less*?

The idea of making professional skills available to the public, as suggested in Chapter 11, is now a matter for action by the Royal Institute of British Architects, which has set up a 'Community

Architecture Working Group' to investigate this very subject. One of the many ideas which the Study will investigate is the possibility of establishing local 'design offices' in which those professionals involved with a given area work within reach of local people. This could go a long way towards breaking up the impersonal, monolithic and remote nature of local Authority professional departments, thus helping to make the resulting schemes much more responsive to local needs and aspirations. However the question of how to pay for making professional services available to local people is still unresolved. It is worth noting, though, that the Royal Town Planning Institute has now decided to permit its members to work for the public free of charge – but not at a reduced fee.

Cautious optimism is justified with regard to some other matters discussed in this book. More murals are being painted (and filmed) in towns throughout the UK, and Michael Norton recently organised a do-it-yourself Mural exhibition in the Institute of Contemporary Arts in London. The Arts Council with the RIBA is organising another 'Art into Landscape' competition (see Chapter 5) this time choosing specific sites which need improvement, the aim being to persuade the local authority to carry out the winning scheme for each site. A second, highly successful '20 ideas for Bristol' exhibition has been held, details of which follow in Case Study 2. The SAVE organisation (see note (c) following) has achieved widespread publicity for its investigations into the links between conservation of buildings and employment and housing, which have been published in *New Society, Built Environment*, and displayed in an exhibition at the Heinz Gallery (dealing specifically with railways and the waste of their building and land resources). Finally the Department of the Environment has granted Inter-Action £15,000 to enable it to assist local groups outside London to set up more City Farms (see Chapter 4) following the success of the Kentish Town Fun Art Farm. Ed Berman reports that vandalism in the area of the Kentish Town Farm has dropped, and that he has had 16 applications for farms elsewhere in the UK. His target for 1977 is to establish at least two of them. The Appendix gives specific details of how such a farm might operate.

Unfortunately, there are few signs that the negative aspects of local authority procedures attacked in this book are abating, as the scarcely edifying story of St Agnes' Place, Lambeth, demonstrates (Case Study Three). Also, it was felt to be a good idea to show how various causes of blight interact with each other, and the article which forms the base of Case Study I was prepared at the suggestion of the *Evening Standard*.

Following the case studies are a few background notes relating to or amplifying points made in the main text.

CASE STUDIES

1 · CAMBERWELL

The difficulty, in identifying and separating the different causes of blight and urban dereliction is that their interaction is not made clear. Blight begets blight, and too much development in a given area can shatter its community feeling to an extent that the community's own self-healing mechanism cannot repair the damage. The following example takes the ancient village of Camberwell in South London, only a few miles from Charing Cross or Victoria. The heart of this community was the Green, and all the items mentioned in this case study are within a half-mile radius of the Green.

Camberwell was one of the many ancient villages within the Greater London boundaries, the head of a large and influential parish – in fact John Ruskin's local centre. When he was alive, it had its Green, Pond, church, shops and Vestry (subsequently Magistrates Court). In the unwritten hierarchy of villages Camberwell stood high, for barely twenty years ago it had its own Music Hall, Lyons Tea Shop, two Grammar Schools, four cinemas, and a thriving shopping centre; making it a far more important place than many of London's other, more famous 'villages'. True, there was a small amount of bomb damage and as in most places there were some areas of overcrowding and insanitary conditions. But in 1957 there was no reason to doubt the future.

Consider Camberwell now. All cinemas closed – two converted to bingo, one to a supermarket, and one standing derelict and shuttered; the Music Hall demolished, its site used for a car lot; the Green strangled by a one-way traffic system which also engulfs a major residential area; a high proportion of shops lying empty and boarded up (with two temporary charity shops); many sites lying derelict and neglected; a shopping street annihilated, its site marked by corrugated sheeting. This pattern of decay and neglect is repeated further away from the Green. So how could this have happened – in barely twenty years?

There were many different and separate causes whose *combined* effect has produced an accelerating decline. First of all, a 20 year redevelopment saga for the so-called central site which contained a church, houses and flats, shops and some industry. The old London County Council was interested in a joint redevelopment with the developers, EPIC, and when, in 1965, it was compelled to hand over planning control for the area to the new Southwark Council, it was on the verge of approving a redevelopment scheme which included a tower-block. Southwark disliked the scheme, which was dropped, and blight has continued for another twelve years, driving businesses, shops and people elsewhere.

On the other side of the Green was Elmington Road, a short, busy shopping street with a newsagent, butcher, confectioner, greengrocer, florist, chemist and about ten market stalls. The road was obliterated to make way for the Magistrates Court and housing development. All shops closed for good, save the chemist which amalgamated with another elsewhere. The stalls may have gone to East Street; but whether or not this was so, it is likely that the economic buoyancy which left Camberwell Green after this treatment went partly up Walworth Road to Camberwell Gate, and partly down to Rye Lane, Peckham. Much of the site of Elmington Road still lies derelict.

Then, in 1964, the London County Council established a one-way traffic scheme around the Green, taking one flank of it through a quiet residential area at the back of the Green, known as Selborne. The aim was to reduce congestion on the main route from Vauxhall Bridge to the A2; but it was at great cost to Camberwell. Since then, the environmental conditions of the Selborne area have deteriorated as heavy long distance traffic thunders between rows of small terrace houses. The decay was further hastened when Southwark Council declared Selborne a redevelopment area in 1969. In 1976, despite last minute injunctions by residents and by the Camberwell Society, the Council began demolition early one Saturday. Yet, a year after defeating the residents in the Courts, the Council has still not managed to demolish all the empty houses, or even to settle on an agreed road plan for the future redevelopment. So the area is part demolished, part occupied, and there is now a possibility that the redevelopment will be shelved as a result of Government cuts. The treatment of the occupants of Selborne was not, and *is* not a credit to any Council. What is more, some 800 people, those living closest to the shops, are being decanted. Even if the redevelopment *does* proceed, the area will not be fully occupied again for at least five years. Yet the 'blight' provisions of the planning acts give no help to shopkeepers who have had their customers removed in this way.

It is surely incredible that the Council cannot organise a phased redevelopment so that part of the area always remains in occupation.

About 1970 the first signs of the Greater London Council's intention to widen part of Camberwell New Road became evident – and the results are still there for all to see – the half burnt, half demolished, late Georgian villas (almost unique in London) whose gutted corpses have been disfiguring the area ever since. Two parts have actually been cleared, and there is apt graffiti on the corrugated iron surrounding one part, saying 'corrugated iron is the character arm of the Council'. There has been no question of allowing these buildings to be used until their demolition is actually needed. Nor even any question that the derelict sites might in the meantime be used for some community purpose. They just lie useless – an appropriate symbol, perhaps, of what is happening to Camberwell as a whole.

There are many other derelict and decayed sites in Camberwell. For example in Church Street, part of the busy through-route, there is a building which has been empty for four years, its windows being left open. Although office use is about the only appropriate use for a building facing such a road, the Council has rejected applications to convert the premises into offices so they remain derelict. Camberwell Grove, opposite, has been undergoing fairly major surgery with the construction of the Lettsom estate – which is now nearing completion. Its construction involved the demolition of a large (substandard) area, the removal of a small factory, and the extinction of the local pub 'The Harrow'. Ironically, a suggestion by the Camberwell Society that the development should be phased, has been taken up in that it has been *completed* in stages: but the area was demolished all at the same time – an empty eyesore for over five years.

Just over the road in Grove Lane, advertisement hoardings hide a large site which has been derelict for almost ten years. It was occupied by a terrace of late Georgian houses when the occupant of one made his front wall collapse during some bathroom alterations. The Council purchased the house and its adjoining houses under slum clearance procedures and gave planning permission to the Utopian Housing Association, for a scheme which the Association did not take up. Negotiations with the Association for a new scheme foundered and the Council-owned site remains derelict. Moreover, because it is not included in the Council's own housing programme, the chances are that this site could remain derelict for many years to come.

On the London side of Camberwell, blight is most obvious as the result of the proposals for London's only 20th century metropolitan-scale park, Burgess Park. A proposal for this was contained in the Greater London Plan of 1943, and its effects are now becoming manifest. In order to create this joyless expanse, houses have been and are being demolished, businesses are being removed from the area, the Surrey Canal has been filled in, and the level of vandalism in this shattered area can be judged from the fact that the only thing to be done with the local (superbly classical) St George's church is that it be reduced to a picturesque ruin. It should be pointed out that this is a GLC proposal, and that Southwark is no longer very enthusiastic about it.

Perhaps as a result of all the foregoing, there is a great deal of simple neglect in Camberwell – neglect of the superb mid Victorian Denmark Hill Station which is becoming increasingly tatty; or British Rail's recent, wanton replacement of fine Victorian railings in Champion Park with chicken wire; or neglect of end-of-terrace sites left growing rose-bay willow-herb, collecting dogs and dumped mattresses; or neglect of the ground level of Council estates, maintained as paltry wedges of grass rather than letting the tenants cultivate them; or even neglect in the Grove, where the Council proposes a gross scheme to replace the front garden areas of a fine row of houses with roadway, concrete paving slabs and bricks instead of restoring the grass and flowers that used to exist there. It is as though the self-respect of the community had finally crumbled after all these combined assaults, like a man ceasing to shave or wash himself.

Blight begets blight. The first mass shifts of population began in the late fifties. The Lyons tea shop closed in the early sixties, followed by the cinemas – one by one – and then the shops. The very extent of rede-velopment, coupled with the dreadful traffic scheme and the extinction of the shopping in Elmington Road has caused a form of social haemor-rhage, leading to a progressive collapse of the community – economically and socially. To add to these disasters, Camberwell is likely to lose its only two secondary schools – Wilson's Grammar School has moved to Carshalton, and Mary Datchelor School is threatened with closure. In sum, the place has been reduced to a traffic junction: no people, shops must be sought up Walworth Road, and cinema and school sought down in Peckham.

To be fair, some slight progress is being made. A Working Party to discuss the future of the Central site was set up some three years ago, on which the Camberwell Society is represented, along with the GLC, Southwark and EPIC, the developers. But progress has been painfully slow, displaying little concern to keep to a timetable. However, once the road pattern is agreed, this should release a good deal of land from blight.

Conclusions

It is very likely that some of these sad developments may be purely the result of changes in social habits, rather than developments peculiar to Camberwell. For example, cinemas closed all over the United Kindom, and it is quite possible that there were insufficient people to sustain four in use. But part of the blame must also rest on the general atmosphere and environment of their location, for seedy and derelict surroundings, with litter strewn pavements are likely to deter people from visiting the cinema.

Equally, the growth in the use of motor vehicles has spelt disaster for many an ancient community which unfortunately straddles a through route, and in Camberwell's case, the people responsible for the revised traffic arrangements may have been unaware of the existence of an ancient village and community centre. Lines on traffic maps do not tend to indicate such wishy-washy matters. There must be those, therefore, to whom the traffic function of Camberwell is vastly more important than its community function; and the thousands of drivers who pass through it every day would probably agree.

The details of this case study underline the extent to which the effects of blight are always local – on the morale of an area, on the economic viability of shops, and on the maintenance of a community spirit. A spell of six months in a house adjacent to a derelict site or empty house would do more good to many a planner or councillor than a host of statistics. As a *Punch* cartoon said recently 'I know there's a telephone box around here. . . . I can smell it!'

Some of the examples mentioned above illustrate the dismal extent of a Council's inability to move quickly in a development, or unwillingness to phase developments so as to produce as little damage to the community as possible. It might be said that Southwark's new Housing Strategy in favour of small developments and rehabilitation (recently approved) will mean that the example of Selborne is never likely to be repeated. But this strategy is not due to take effect until the early 1980s, and there still remain in the Council's programme the other communities clearances, most notably that of Nunhead.

Finally, there is an obvious point to be made. It is that those vested with the guardianship of this community and others like it – namely the local authorities – have insufficiently understood all the different and interlocking considerations which go to make up a community; and that by concentrating on two sub-factors, such as traffic and rehousing, they have come perilously close to killing Camberwell altogether.

2 · 20 IDEAS FOR BRISTOL

The second of the exhibitions with this title was held during November and December 1976 in the Bristol Museum and Art Gallery, in a room specially prepared for this purpose. The organisers estimate that it was visited by upwards of 15,000 people, and they have been invited to organise another similar exhibition in eighteen months.The exhibition was organised by six people who invited other individuals or groups to prepare a display, thus reducing the load on the organisers themselves. In this second exhibition, contributors ranged from architects, designers, the City and County planning departments to simply interested individuals, pressure groups such as the Friends of the Earth, and to a 'Community Architecture' scheme prepared for the Kite area in Cambridge by architect Keith Garbett.

The absence of a rigid format produced a visual variety in the exhibition which more than matched the splendid variety of the suggestions. These ranged from proposals to re-use empty houses, rejuvenate the Bristol Docks area, establish community food stores, create a riverside walkway along the Avon, paint murals on the sides of large buildings, to re-opening the railway line from Bristol to Portishead. This particular exhibit was one of the most imaginative I have ever seen in an exhibition. A complete railway carriage compartment was erected in the exhibition room (genuine nostalgia for British Railways) and a back-projected slide screen filled its window space. As you sat in this carriage, a series of slides showed the views you would see if you were in a railway carriage travelling along this particular line. The scenery is spectacular, since the line runs along the bottom of the Avon Gorge. The proposition is that the railway should re-open as a travelling restaurant which would travel very slowly up and down this line.

Some discussion has been caused by querying the purpose of such an exhibition: is it just for fun, or is it intended that the schemes should be built? At this stage the organisers intend to limit their intention to the sole aim of inspiring others to take up some of the ideas. Indeed, some of those proposed in the first exhibition are now being implemented: a town trail has been prepared by Sue Jones, the Council is preparing a walkway along the banks of the Avon, and people have begun to cultivate allotments on previously neglected land. Many of the ideas in the exhibition are Bristol variants of projects which have been discussed in this book, which *could* be undertaken by local people without too much difficulty. The problem is one of translating a good idea into reality, and inspiring other people to take the initiative.

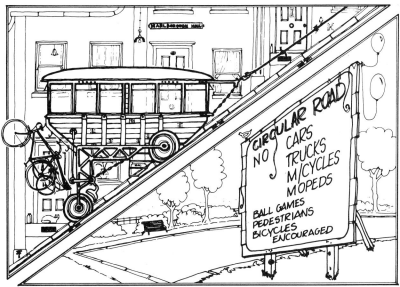

Illustrations from the '20 Ideas for Bristol' exhibition

BRISTOL   PILL   PORTISHEAD

THIS NEGLECTED RAILWAY
COULD BE USED FOR SUMMER
EVENING AND WEEKEND
STEAM HAULED PLEASURE TRIPS.

A TRAIN OF FIRST CLASS COACHES,
WITH FULL RESTAURANT SERVICE,
WOULD GIVE BRISTOLIANS
A CHANCE TO TRAVEL AT A
LEISURELY PACE DOWN THE
SPECTACULAR AVON GORGE,
WHILST ENJOYING A GOOD MEAL.

3 · *ST AGNES PLACE, LAMBETH*

St Agnes Place is a street of large, terraced, Victorian houses which separate Kennington Park from East Kennington Park. Since statistics indicated that the surrounding area is one which is deficient in parks, the Council had a long-standing ambition to demolish St Agnes Place so that the two Kennington Parks could be amalgamated in a single, reasonably sized, well-provided park. However, there are over 17,000 people on this Council's housing list, and 49 large houses are not an asset to be squandered. The threat of redevelopment had caused many of the indigenous inhabitants to move away over some years, leaving houses either empty, or occupied by squatters – several of whom carried out repair work to the buildings in which they were living. As the day for demolition approached, some of the inhabitants (helped by some councillors) tried to reverse the decision by asking Tom Woolley and Colin Taylor of the Architectural Association to carry out a structural survey of the houses. The survey indicated that all, bar a few, were sound enough to be rehabilitated. However, the Council refused to reconsider its decision, and very early on January 19 1977 demolition began, the workmen being protected by the police. Just before 11.00 am, an injunction to stop the demolition was issued by the High Court after an application by some Lambeth ratepayers. The final outcome is not known.

There is one significant point in this sorry tale: it is the admission by the Council that even once the houses are demolished, there is insufficient money to pay for creating the site into a park, for the time being. To reduce habitable houses to a grassed-over space at ground level is a waste of scarce resources of truly alarming proportions.

4 · *AN INNER LONDON CO-OPERATIVE*

This case study clearly illustrates some of the points brought out in the main book regarding professional advice for the public, local organisation, and the relationship with a large local authority.

The location of the Co-operative is a short street close to central London consisting of some 36, three-storey terraced houses, constructed nearly a hundred years ago. About half of these houses are owned by absentee owners, two are owned by the local Council and the remainder are owned by owner-occupiers most of whom have tenants. The character of the area is not pretty: a major road to the west; industry hemming in on one side and an old, run down council estate on the other. The houses themselves suffer from certain defects, the most important being their narrow site causing poor lighting to the rooms on the ground and first floors, at the rear. The residents do not wish to have the street named in case speculators purchase the houses from the absentee owners, thus forcing the prices to rise.

The local Council declared this street a Clearance Area under Part III of the 1957 Housing Act, but the residents – both tenants and owner-occupiers – were unwilling to move. At a Public Inquiry, the proposal was opposed by a Residents Association (representing both tenants and owner-occupiers) and by an architect/planner, Chris Whittaker, who had been retained by a number of owner-occupiers on the basis of the experience Whittaker had gained in such cases elsewhere in London. The Inspector recommended clearance of the houses, but the Secretary of State dissented. In his decision (early 1976), the Secretary of State accepted that although the houses had 'defects that cannot be corrected by rehabilitation' and must remain in some respects substandard, he still concluded that the most satisfactory course was to improve them for the resident community whose 'vigorous community spirit' had impressed him.

The owner-occupiers managed to raise £200 initially to meet Whittaker's fee for fighting their case at the public enquiry; and they have been able to recover the whole of it from public funds as successful statutory objectors.

With the help and support of the local Action Centre, the tenants have set up a Co-operative whose aim is to manage the rehabilitation of these homes. Firstly, the freeholds have to be purchased by the GLC (which has undertaken to do this) and they will lease the houses to the Co-operative and fund their repair and conversion. The Co-operative is in the process of registering as a Housing Association for this purpose. The registered Housing Association for this area is the Quadrant Housing Association which, far from impeding the new Association, proffered early advice and assistance.

Work has begun on compiling a rehabilitation programme, which will cover 20 of the 36 houses. Some 76 people now live in these 20 houses, 58 of whom have declared their wish to remain, and the plan is to convert the 20 houses into 50 units. The work will be helped by the fact that the local Council (which has now made friends with the Co-operative) has offered the two empty houses in their ownership to the Co-operative, and it will thus be possible for people to stay in these houses whilst their own are being rehabilitated. As was the experience in Black Road, Macclesfield, some of the residents of this street are in building trades, but no decision has yet been made as to how the work shall be carried out. There is concern that something, at any rate, should be manifest as soon as the freehold passes to the GLC, if only to increase morale.

Whittaker would like the main builders to start the day after the purchase has been completed, but that depends upon the speed of approvals. In the meantime, the Council is prepared to serve notices on owners where urgent repairs are necessary, and, in one case, it is about to repair a badly leaking roof and recover the cost from the absentee landlord.

The difference between this scheme and the Black Road scheme is that Whittaker is not a resident, living on the site, but a professional called in for his expertise. Consequently, some of the day-to-day problems which Rod Hackney was able to solve in Black Road, because he lived there, are escaping Whittaker. But he and a resident architect now have the prospect of a conventional commission from a client – the Co-operative – which had only come into existence as a result of the residents' determination and the architect's conviction.

Notes

(a) *Housing Corporation procedures.* A flat recently created in the roof space of a house illustrates one way in which Housing Corporation procedures may inhibit rather than encourage the provision of more homes. The architect claimed that the flat (in which he had decided to live) would not be acceptable by the Housing Corporation because:

(a) The bedrooms opened off the living room
(b) The kitchen opened off the living room
(c) The lavatory/bathroom was downstairs from the bedrooms
(d) A spiral staircase had been used.

The reason for these restrictions is that flats designed like that could cause problems for certain types of households, and Housing Associations often (or usually) dislike nominating tenants in advance for a particular flat. The consequence is that the cost of Housing Association flats increases considerably, since provision must be made for corridors, off which the various rooms can open. When converting older buildings this requirement for corridors can often vitiate a good scheme, and turn a large flat into a pokey one.

(b) *Local Authority Liability.* Many of the regulations mentioned in chapter 10 are being made more stringent year after year, as the direct result of the theory of local Authority responsibility. This theory, probably emanating from the USA, makes the local Authority legally responsible for virtually everything in its area – from the safety of houses to the absence of potholes. The converse is that if anything happens to you – from twisting your ankle in a pothole to being hit on the head by a falling balcony – you can sue the local Authority. Naturally, if the local Authority is to face bills for damages on the scale such a theory implies, then it will raise the necessary standards to avoid the possibility of being sued. The result is that buildings constructed to these high standards are too expensive for people to be able to afford to live in them. If the application of standards is to become more flexible, then a new ruling on local Authority liability is required. It would be no bad thing if building owners and their professional advisers became responsible for their own buildings; and that people who fall into potholes should be told to look where they are going.

(c) *The Save Organisation.* To coincide with European Architectural Heritage Year, the 'Save Britain's Heritage' campaign was organised, to highlight historic buildings which, despite the new preoccupation with conservation, were in danger of being demolished. Since its first report (in the *Architect's Journal* December 1975), the organisation has greatly widened its sphere of investigation. Recent reports include one on *Conservation and Shops*, which demonstrates the link between the fate of small businesses and employment; *The Concrete Jerusalem*, which investigates the fate of town centres and how life has been driven out of them; and *Off the Rails*, which investigates British Rail, and its policy toward railway stations. This volunteer organisation is carrying out unpaid research work of considerable importance, in the absence of any interest in these subjects from official bodies; moreover, its reports explode the myth that conservation is the preserve of the rich élite. It demonstrates conclusively that conservation means, in its widest sense, the *best use of existing resources*, and that this affects rich and poor, antique shop and die-stamping factory, poor flats and expensive private houses alike.

Worth reading

The Concrete Jerusalem (SAVE Report) New Society. 30 December 1976.
Conservation and Jobs (SAVE Report) Built Environment. September 1976.
The Save Report Architect's Journal. January 1976.
Off the Rails (SAVE Report) £1 from SAVE, 3 Park Square West, London NW1.
Shelter Report: Another Empty Home. 40p from Shelter.

APPENDIX

City Farm Land Bank Brochure

The City Farm Land Bank will attempt to obtain the use of waste land in cities throughout the United Kingdom for medium term and long-term facilities of a City Farm nature. The land is intended to be held in Trust by Town & Country Inter-Action Trust under licence or lease at a nominal rent whenever possible.

Major sources of this land are expected to be local authorities, British Rail, and other public authorities. The land will be returned to the freeholders as and when their own development schemes come into effect.

The City Farm Land Bank will act as a clearing house and advisory service for self-help facilities on such waste land. This experienced service will minimise bureaucracy and will guarantee the proper management of leases and licences. A basic goal for every project will be to have local management groups chosen from the adults and teenagers who make use of the facilities.

WHY

It is a sound use of wasted land

It involves minimal capital expenditure

Because there is little construction work required for these farm-type facilities, the land can be obtained from and revert to freeholders without great fears on their part.

The rural finish gives a mimimal target for vandalism.

Projects can be largely self-supporting by offering unique facilities otherwise unavailable to Inner City areas.

Because the workers do not have to protect buildings, they can concentrate on programme development.

Whatever other activities are started on a City Farm, there is bound to be one or more of the following: gardening, horses or domesticated animals. These three areas are of great interest to all age groups throughout the UK, but opportunities to participate in them are inadequate in cities.

Because of this universal appeal, real community-based facilities can be set up involving adults and young people side by side, each with their own management committee.

The first City Farm has proved the case sufficiently to try it elsewhere through the Land Bank. City Farm I is also self-supporting. Run by a voluntary group, it was built in six months by voluntary labour and donations in kind from local firms. It did not cost the ratepayers a single penny. It simply required a licence for the waste land and planning permission for temporary structures.

On the three acres of City Farm I the following are found:

A community garden for the elderly (flowers and market gardening on a sharing basis)

An indoor riding school (renovated out of a derelict timber shed)

Stables, tack room, hay shed, store room and caretaker's flat (renovated out of derelict out-buildings)

Auto-repair workshop (built out of scrap materials)

Animal pens (built out of castaway wood from a building site – animals donated)

Allotments (built on reclaimed land and former BR Allotment Land)

Compost, manure, and other re-cycling activities

Household repair workshop, tea room, meeting/rehearsal room, pottery and leather workshop (in renovated workshop)

Picnic area

Possible Daily Programme

A City Farm might only be one acre or it might have up to fifty; it might have only one of the above facilities, such as a community garden, or allotments or a farmyard, or it might have a combination of two or more; it needn't have all the facilities.

A typical daily programme on City Farm I includes all of the above being used in different ways by different age groups.

School parties visit the hand-reared animals. They might also participate in drama or arts and crafts workshops related to the animals or have lectures, films, etc. Children are given follow-up materials to take away. These visits are a source of income for the farm but cost less than most other school visits.

Pony Clubs for local children from local housing estates meet after school for riding lessons; Youth Clubs come in the evening handicapped riding takes place on the weekends. Special schools, normal schools and truant projects use the stables during school hours.

The weekend in warm weather gives an ideal opportunity for picnics, fetes, as well as mixing handicapped and able-bodied children together through drama and music activities centred around the animals. Many charities are interested in the community integration of the handicapped which City Farms are uniquely placed to do.

One of the key features of the farms is that adults can use them for their own activities from gardening to household repairs to auto repairs. Thus, instead of dividing people up in different institutions, the City Farm attempts to allow a set of community activities to take place naturally, side by side, with adults taking responsibility for their own neighbourhood children.

City Farm I is a project base for youth employment and training projects as well as similar projects for the elderly. These take many forms from learning the economics of egg and goat-milk production, to training in community work and play leadership, to training in motor mechanics, woodwork, etc.

City Farms can be self-supporting by saving local authorities money. For example, by giving riding lessons at a lower rate than commercial establishments which are usually out of city centres requiring travel costs as well. There are many ways in which ratepayers' money can be saved by turning waste land into community facilities like City Farms.

A NOTE ON SOURCES

Although most of this book is based on original investigation, some of it is a compilation (in a different form) of material published elsewhere, and the key sources are listed below.

Building Design a weekly newspaper for the Building Industry, which has featured an excellent series of articles on self-help, warehouse conversions and solar technology.

Architectural Design (AD) a very useful series of articles on self-build and housing improvements – particularly the August 1976 issue (articles by Tom Woolley).

Planning Magazine an invaluable weekly newspaper which charts how our world is being changed for us, including a series of planning appeal decisions illustrating the horrifying extent to which our private life has become a matter for public legislation.

Community Action an overtly political bi-monthly magazine, which is a first-class source of information about the law, public enquiries, and housing legislation, including a useful page describing new (often local) publications and reports which never hit the headlines.

Bulletin of Environmental Education (BEE) edited by Colin Ward and published by the Town and Country Planning Association – mainly aimed at teachers, but with interesting ideas for projects.

The number of unofficial and voluntary publications is most impressive and too great to list here: however, one deserves special mention: *In the Making* (a directory of proposed productive projects in self-management), 35p from 221 Albert Road, Sheffield, is the modern co-operative movement's answer to Samuel Smiles' *Self-Help*.

INDEX